A REBEL IN GAZA

Asmaa al-Ghoul
and Selim Nassib

A Rebel in Gaza

Behind the Lines of the Arab Spring,

One Woman's Story

Translated from the French by

Mike Mitchell

DoppelHouse Press | Los Angeles

Cet ouvrage a bénéficié du soutien des Programmes d'aide à la publication de l'Institut français. / This work, published as part of a program of aid for publication, received support from the Institute Français.

Cover design: Kourosh Beigpour
Typesetting: Carrie Paterson and Jody Zellen

Publisher's Cataloging-in-Publication data

Names: al-Ghoul, Asmaa, author. | Nassib, Sélim, author. | Mitchell, Mike, translator.
Title: A Rebel in Gaza : behind the lines of the Arab Spring, one woman's story /
Asmaa al-Ghoul and Selim Nassib ; translated from the French by Mike Mitchell.
Description: Los Angeles, CA: Doppelhouse Press, 2018.
Identifiers: ISBN 9780998777023 (Hardcover) | 9780998777054 (pbk.) |
9780998777085 (ebook) | LCCN 2018937177
Subjects: LCSH al-Ghoul, Asmaa. | Palestinian Arabs--Biography. | Women,
Palestinian Arab--Biography. | Feminists--Gaza Strip--Biography. | Journaists--Gaza
Strip--Biography. | Arab-Israeli conflict. | Women--Gaza Strip--Social conditions. |
Women and war--Gaza Strip. | BISAC BIOGRAPHY & AUTOBIOGRAPHY / Women |
BIOGRAPHY & AUTOBIOGRAPHY / Editors, Journalists, Publishers | BIOGRAPHY
& AUTOBIOGRAPHY / Personal Memoirs | BIOGRAPHY & AUTOBIOGRAPHY /
Social Activists | HISTORY / Middle East / Israel & Palestine | POLITICAL SCIENCE /
Human Rights | POLITICAL SCIENCE / World / Middle Eastern
Classification: LCC DS110.G3 A576 2018 | LCC 956.94/05/0924

DoppelHouse Press | Los Angeles, California

To the Rafah refugee camp
that my grandparents built
and that in turn gave birth to me,
the scene of my first smile.

Contents

Preface by Selim Nassib

A Woman Emerging from an Alley...

S HE SUDDENLY EMERGES from an alley in Cairo and flings her arms around your neck. You don't know her, you've never seen her before. The man she's with has told her who you are and she's run over to you; her laugh enfolds you, her eyes are shining, she's looking at you, searching for something you once wrote about Umm Kulthum that she liked, or something else, a detail, some sign that tells her you're one of her people, one of those to whom she can talk freely.

It was toward the end of 2011, the pulse of the Arab Spring was still beating. Asmaa al-Ghoul, a Palestinian writer from Gaza, was staying temporarily in Cairo to keep out of the public eye for a while. Some years previously she had publicly opposed her uncle, a commander in the Hamas forces, more or less accusing him of being an assassin in an open letter posted on the internet. A further reason for this voluntary move away: the exhausting pressure she was subjected to day after day and which, oddly enough, surprised her. For what she writes is infused with a kind of ingenuousness, the innocent expression of an inner feeling of rebellion against the enforced islamization, the so-called crimes of honor, the sexist segregation... It's not her fault that her nature is in all respects incompatible with the stifling regime prevailing in Gaza. A Muslim, a believer if non-practicing, it would be very wrong to define her solely by her opposition to Hamas. She cannot find words scathing enough to denounce the boundless corruption of Fatah, the criminal inhumanity of Israel—and her criticism extends to the human rights organizations, the feminist movements, the international institutions, Europe, the United States, all of whom are more or less complicit in a corrupt system which ultimately keeps things as they are. With whom, then, does she side? With the humble folk, the rebels, the ordinary, anonymous people of Gaza. Confronted with the all-pervading male chauvinism, besieged and bombarded by Israel, subjected to the obscurantist regime of Hamas, she is at the focal point of all possible oppression in the Arab world—and her vibrant energy absorbs and rejects them all.

The ordinary little restaurant to which she drags me off is in a narrow rising passageway with the tables on the steps. The kitchen's out in the open air, the cook is a friend of hers. Asmaa al-Ghoul makes friends easily and talks to everyone in the same way. She has a natural ease and exuberance which allows her to say what she thinks without seeming aggressive.

Childhood in the Rafah refugee camp, first Intifada at five, Israeli soldiers hammering on the door in the middle of the night, uncles joining Hamas and imposing its moral order at home, father often absent (he works in the Emirates) but tolerant, keen on reading, writing... She tells me everything, and her portrait is in the first issue of *L'Impossible*, the magazine launched in Paris by Michel Butel. She says, "I think the real occupying forces are the internal ones, Hamas, Fatah, the parties... then comes the major occupation: Israel. We can't get rid of the latter without first of all getting rid of the former. To be honest, we are being subjected to a siege of the mind that is much more important than the siege on the borders."

She returns to Gaza and continues to follow this nuanced radical line which makes her into a target from all sides, but she just can't change. She gets blows and death threats; she is put in prison, where the Hamas policewomen hit her with the aim of turning her into a 'good Muslim'; she remains one of the rare Gazan women who refuse to cover their heads because they haven't read anything in the Koran that obliges them to. This inability to compromise even affects her private life, especially her relationships with men: just thirty years old and her two marriages have both ended in divorce.

She keeps saying that she isn't heroic, that she has no desire to be so. Her dream, still unfulfilled, is to be an ordinary woman, to have a husband, children, a quiet life, love—but that is a fantasy beyond her grasp, an aspiration quickly thwarted by her fiery temperament, her inability to submit. She no longer has any desire to be a 'militant', she refuses the appellation of 'feminist'; her activity as a journalist takes her away from her vocation of writer. She is still trying to find her way in literature even though her first collection of short stories, *Séparation sur un tableau noir* (Segregation on a Blackboard), was well received. Her second, *La Ville de l'amour et du péché* (The City of Love and Sin), is still too 'realist' for her; she refuses to hand it over to her publisher in that state.

Starting with that first meeting in the restaurant on the steps there was tacit understanding between us. But the book we planned to write together came up against practical problems. Go and see her in Gaza? The military regime that has established itself in Cairo again has closed its border with the enclave, and Israel's invariable reply to my request for a transit visa is that it is 'under consideration'—it still is today. Invite her to come to France? Her suitcase is quickly packed—but the border remains closed week after week. I really come to understand what 'Gaza, the open-air prison' means. But everything works out: one day she manages to get into Egypt and takes the plane. In a house in Normandy she starts talking again, under the eyes of grazing cows, and doesn't stop. She speaks in Arabic, I write it down in French—then she gets me to translate it all back. What she describes is the daily life of a society run by Hamas: how people fall in love, get married, suffer repeated wars, go down to the beach, cycle, smoke their hookahs under that yoke. She responds point by point to their claim to subject life to a stupid order. Or rather it is she herself, the woman she is, her Islam, the nuances of her thought, the very possibility of her existing that are the reply to the Islamism that reigns supreme. This 'daughter of Gaza' doesn't just talk superficially and her criticism is not theoretical: she pulls a thread and everything comes. She doesn't claim to have a solution to offer but simply bears witness to the fact that she and those of her generation who are like her are very much alive. At least so far.

She stops talking and goes back to Gaza, only to be caught up in the war of summer 2014. She covers it for an online newspaper based in Washington, *Al Monitor*, dashing from one end of the territory to the other, writing every day, braving the danger like any other of her fellow journalists. The missiles from the Israeli fighters don't hit her but instead the house where she spent her childhood: nine members of her family, including a baby and her sixty-year-old uncle, die in the explosion and not one of them had any links with Hamas. She pours out her sorrow in an article that has remained famous: "Never ask me about peace again." Less than twenty-four hours later she's collected herself and writes on her Facebook page, "It's a new day starting... You have to let your wounds heal... care for the bereaved and the refugees."

She comes back to Paris to relate the last twists of the story before returning home again. It's March 2015, the manuscript of *A Rebel in Gaza* is finally ready. She just has to come back to France for the launch of the book.

That is the beginning of a long wait punctuated by constant requests for a transit visa from the Israeli, Egyptian and Jordanian authorities... She won a British award for the defense of human rights, but the UK authorities refused her an entry visa. The US embassy gained permission from the Israeli authorities to allow her access to the West Bank to take part in a conference. She goes there, makes an emotional visit to Jerusalem and assumes she can now cross into Jordan and take the plane from Amman. But the Jordanian authorities inform her by SMS that she is not allowed to cross the border—don't ask me why! She hears that a group of artists and writers from Gaza have been invited to take part in a cultural event in Paris and Marseilles; she tries to join them, but too late: the request for a collective transit visa has already been sent off... and accepted. In the meantime her request for an entry visa to the Schengen area has already expired, she has to get all the documents together again to renew her application. The border with Egypt is only open for three days, the number she has been allocated would allow her to cross... on the fourth. And that without mentioning all the strain on her private life this perpetual confinement inevitably causes. Along with the other 1.8 million inhabitants of Gaza, Asmaa finds herself a prisoner in the territory for fourteen months! The Egyptian president, Sissi, and the Israeli prime minister, Netanyahu, claim they are suppressing Hamas, when all the relentless blockade is doing is to strengthen it and allow it to continue the enforced islamization of Gaza society in isolation. "Books, films, music, all those things that are so important, are few and far between for the children of Gaza," she writes.

"And they are the things that transform people, they are what transformed me! How can we judge those who have never had access to them? This criminal conservatism is entirely founded on illusions, fantasies, the discourse of the parties, the mosques or the government... But if you look inside someone, what do you see? All they need is a good book. That's what's lacking in Gaza, nothing else. All this territory needs is to open itself up to the world—it's the siege imposed by Israel, Hamas and Egypt that stops that from happening."

It is a strange fact that the external world seems to think that Gaza, with all the destruction, the blockade and suffering, doesn't quite belong to the same planet. They are moved by it a little when war is raging, admitting that it is inhuman to punish a people collectively because they are led by islamists; then they forget. The summer 2014 war had hardly finished when people in Israel were already talking about the next; it was enough for a few rockets to be launched at the wrong (or perhaps the right) moment. But a new war to accomplish what? To 'mow the grass,' is the reply of *Breaking the Silence*, an association of Israeli soldiers hostile to the occupation, taking up the phrase used by their superior officers for the strategy of returning again and again in order to cut down the 'weeds' growing in their backyard.

Then suddenly, on the occasion of Ramadan 2016, Egypt decides to open the border for five days, publishing the numbers of those who will be authorized to pass through. With her number of 10962 Asmaa realizes that she would be one of them. Starting at five in the morning, her progress resembles an obstacle race, with anxiety and humiliation at each stage for all the unfortunate travelers. Finally, after a thousand twists and turns, she arrives in Cairo at midnight, where she can once more connect up with the world, with the airlines, with the free air.

So *A Rebel in Gaza* comes to us in the present, not having lost anything of its topicality because time in the enclave is more or less at a standstill. It is as if we were listening to this young woman wondering whether her voice, speaking out against the general trend, will fall silent without provoking a response or not. The situation in the region is hardly favorable to it. Almost everywhere the Arab Spring has been crushed in repression that has led to horrors, slaughter, civil wars—as if, menaced by chaos, the people had no other choice than that between the military and islamists. Despite herself, Asmaa al-Ghoul continues to say what she has to say—and to look on the world, as far as possible through the eyes of a free woman.

October 2016

Foreword

As If I've Been Alive for a Long Time

IT WAS DIFFICULT for me to write about Gaza. With all the political and ideological conflicts in the territory, to write a history that would be accepted by all was not that easy—but at least it was my own story I was telling, and my voice did not claim to speak in the name of anyone else. The most awkward aspect was to keep away from the prevailing clichés, from the ode to the liberation of the occupied land or the story of a young woman standing up to the government on her own. On the contrary, I wanted to be at the heart of stories of everyday life, of those that avoid the headlines, to present an account that might shock readers accustomed to the usual political clichés.

To put it simply, this book only became a credible undertaking at the moment I met the Franco-Lebanese writer Selim Nassib in the Altak'iba Café in Cairo. I told him how much I admired his book on Umm Kulthum and suggested we write one together. Then the decisive moment came when the publisher Mireille Paolini put this book in process. The three of us then worked on a project that was hardly easy and took more than four years. Every time we had to meet for the next stage it meant that I had to spend a long time waiting at the border between Gaza and Egypt until the barrier was raised. Or I kept an eye on the border with Israel, hoping my Israeli transit visa would arrive—which in fact never actually happened. I was having to live in hope that we could meet again and write a further chapter during endless discussions or have a session on Skype. That, for me, was more difficult than taking an exam at school.

Lost in Translation—the title of that film kept coming back to mind during the writing or discussions, but after each paragraph and each page we made sure that there was no such loss of meaning. Often love, mourning, stories of fatherhood, motherhood, marriage, betrayal, war and death demanded not so much a translator as a writer of fine sensitivity. It is the heart that translates life and lays it out on paper, and that is what Selim does with every word, every thought, every expression. Not getting caught up in the event and avoiding journalese was the other challenge we had to face so that the writing remained literary and personal. Of course, the account remained basically political and journalistic but at the same time it was done so as to live on inside us for years.

The city of Gaza is abuzz with such a profusion of love, happiness, death and oppression that it prevents you from seeing other places. As if all the other places in the world, even modern, developed towns, were cut off from it. As if the sufferings of Gaza extended my life and made me feel the inverse of the feeling expressed by Keats, "I have an habitual feeling of my real life having passed, and that I am leading a posthumous existence."

For life in Gaza has a strength that makes you feel that death doesn't exist, except in war. And that your life will continue until the time when the problems of power outages, of reconciliation between Fatah and Hamas, or of reconstruction have been resolved. Or that it will remain in a state of suspension, as if the city were keeping another life in reserve for you while waiting for its problems to be settled. And thus it is that Gaza draws you to her and binds you to your native soil, as if she were the center of the universe. And you wait, and you wait...

And it is in this hope, in the expectation of this change, of this love, of these kindhearted people that this book was born.

Asmaa al-Ghoul

October 2016

1

You'll End Up in the Fire

WHEN WE WERE CHILDREN, one of our favorite games was Arabs and Jews. Some would hide while the others looked for them. In general the boys were the Jews and we, the girls, the Arabs. Because the Jews were stronger and more brutal. No one thought about what that meant; we weren't interested in politics, the important thing was to have fun. We really loved that game. Normally we played it out in the street—when there was no curfew, that is.

In Rafah Camp, where I grew up, we never said "the Israelis," nor even "the army," we said, "the Jews," for example "The Jews are coming!" For me "Jew" meant fear. At night, sleeping on a mattress on the ground, I would think about the bombardments, about death, about the planes flying over, tearing off the roofs. I would look at the big yellow tin of Nido powdered milk on top of the closet. It was the most valuable thing one could get in that Camp—the common run of people drank the unbranded milk from UNRWA, the United Nations agency that deals with the Palestinian refugees. I would say to myself, "Oh my God, why aren't I a tin of Nido?" Everyone respected it. They would take it down to put a spoonful in their tea and then replace it. It was looked on with esteem, while I spent my days hearing people say to me, "You'll end up in the fire, you'll go to hell." Of course, I was convinced I was going to burn in the flames.

The soldiers would always barge in by the back door, the one to my room. Sometimes I would wake with a start, "Mama, Mama, the Jews are coming, I can hear their boots." She would reply, "No, no, it's the sound of the alarm clock... You go back to sleep." The patter of the raindrops on the corrugated-iron roof, the tick-tock of the alarm clock, the soldiers bursting in—those three things are forever intermingled for me. My whole life was trapped within those moments of fear and sadness. When you're happy you're always expecting something happy to *turn up*—but that doesn't often occur. Sadness is more constant, it suits my character better, it harmonizes with it. When the first Intifada broke out, in 1987, I was only five, but I still have the smell of the tear-gas in my nostrils. Hamas was founded in the same year; I grew up with it. It was a world that was both stable and sad. My uncles were members of Hamas, that's why the Israelis would come bursting in on us in the middle of the night, terrorizing me.

However, I had been to Israel when I was little. Grandfather Jomaa, my father's father, worked in a hotel there—which had helped him to get admitted to a hospital in Tel Aviv when he had heart problems. I was taken there to visit him. The bus stopped at a service station and the pump attendant had started to clean the windows by spraying them. The water came out of the pipe and splattered on the glass, making it look rippled. I was afraid and started to cry. At the hospital I went up in an elevator for the first time in my life. When the door opened, the décor was completely different, I couldn't understand it. I asked my grandmother, "Have we been on a journey, *Teta*? Have we been on a journey in this... this..." I didn't even know that it was called an elevator! A little later we were sitting on the hospital lawn. All that green around us—I couldn't believe my eyes! In the

Camp, where I'd grown up, there was no greenery *at all*. With me, my grandfather was looking at all the women stretched out, heads bare, on the grass together with their families: "That one has cancer, that one has a heart condition... Over there it's her children who've come to see her." In that garden I discovered that the Jews were perfectly ordinary people. I still couldn't believe they really were Jews. It was hearing them speak Hebrew that convinced me. Until then I thought that all Jews were soldiers.

That grandfather was an open-minded man. He taught me tolerance towards other peoples. Before I was born, he had invited my father to have a holiday in Israel. He bore no hatred whatsoever and found it normal that his son should learn Hebrew. He talked about his Israeli boss with great respect and appreciated his own work—in charge of the hotel bellhops. He showed me photographs taken in Tel Aviv of himself and my grandmother in a beautiful dress with her bracelets, hair blowing in the wind. Some of his children had joined Hamas, but not him. On the one hand he lived among the soldiers who attacked his house; on the other beside his boss, whom he liked very much. He would come back from Israel with cakes that tasted different, with a whole pile of delicious things. And he would give me a half-shekel pocket money. That was a lot. The girls at school got a hundredth of a half-shekel. At that time anyone who worked in Israel was regarded as rich.

Despite all that, I preferred my other grandfather, Abdullah, my mother's father. He had also taken us to Israel, to a farm where he worked as a laborer, the most marvelous trip in my life! There were innumerable birds in the sky. We started to sing for them *The bird of Thursday brought me a shirt*—in Arabic "Thursday" rhymes with "shirt." He got us to pick some plants that we took back home. I really loved him. One day when it was raining in Rafah, we were sitting underneath his olive tree and I suddenly had the same feeling as I had when he read the Koran out loud. At that very moment a pigeon shat on me—that's the way things always are with me. But my grandfather said, "Don't let it bother you, it brings luck. You're going to get some good news."

People say "the Gaza Strip" (or "Gaza") to designate the territory, but "Gaza" is also the name of the capital. If Israel was a different world for us, so was the city of Gaza. The first time I went there I was flabbergasted because I came from the Rafa refugee camp, some forty kilometers to the south where there was nothing. I was entering a world that was so vast it was impossible to get to know it completely. That day my aunt took me to a wedding among the upper classes of Gaza and I just stood and stared: a luxury villa surrounded by trees, a garage for the cars, men in dark suits, elegant women, bareheaded and their faces uncovered. So there were people who were rich—and Palestinian! I couldn't get over it. I was well dressed, for my father always sent me nice clothes from the Emirates, where he worked. I was wearing a floral hat and I suddenly realized I'd left it in the shared taxi. Furious, I went to find the driver, "You went off with my hat, you beast!" And the poor guy had just returned to give it back to me. I wasn't even five and I was already unbearable.

2

Too Strong-Minded

I LOVED BOYS, especially good-looking boys. I always preferred to play with them rather than with the little girls who hated me because I was "too strong-minded." It's a description that has followed me my whole life.

At sixteen, on my return from the Emirates, I fell in love with a cousin who put his hand on my shoulder—and my heart started to beat as never before. I had no idea that a hand on your shoulder could provoke such overwhelming sensations. His mother had spread the rumor that I went out onto the balcony in shorts and with my arms uncovered—a blatant lie. She also managed to separate us. I wasn't the right woman for her son, I was "too strong-minded."

The same accusation was also made a little later when at seventeen I fell in love with an English teacher of twenty-four. He was called Saleh. It was an odd relationship. He taught in a different class from mine so that we had no pretext to speak to each other. We would run into each other in the school corridors, he would say a few words to me, I would reply furtively and we would continue on our separate ways. I quivered when our eyes met, when I slipped a poem I'd written into his hand or he slipped me one of his. It was all a matter of words snatched in passing, glances exchanged from a distance. I didn't dare go any farther because I was afraid of gossip, but I was thinking about him all the time. It kept me awake at night. Eventually my father realized I was in love with that teacher; I don't know whether someone told him or he figured it out because I was starting to get poor grades. He went to the school and, on the pretext of finding out how I was doing, he met him: "Since Asmaa's known you her results have gone down. Keep away from her."

Saleh told him, "I want to get engaged to her."

Papa said, "Okay then. We'll see you at our house next Thursday."

He'd decided to refuse him but had invited him to see how serious his intentions were and to have me witness it. The next Thursday, after having tidied up the house and prepared the drinks, we sat there waiting... but he didn't come. His mother was an awful woman, a teacher herself, at an elementary school, and she hated me: "Asmaa will never suit you, she's much too strong-minded." As for men, it seems they weren't strong-minded enough to resist their mothers.

I've been told that Jews and Muslims require their women to cover their heads because of the fear they inspire, because to show one's hair is considered to be sexually pro-vocative. I have also been told that in the history of humanity woman is the basis of life, the mother of the universe. Men have always feared her power and have disguised their 'fear *of* her' in their 'fear *for* her'. In order to protect themselves, they have confined her to the house and reduced her role to a strict minimum, making their religions perpetuate this structure of domination which wasn't originally part of them. That is why a woman's place is inferior and why her children take the name of their father rather than hers. I find this theory convincing. In Gaza there are more women with qualifications than men, but no one encourages the women to look for work and the labor market remains pre-dominantly male. Did the man who was in love with me obey his mother because he was afraid of her? And me, do I make men afraid?

My sister Fatmeh was born in 1983, Aïcha in 1984, Mustafa in 1985 and so on... until there were nine of us. I was the eldest and the family expected me to look after my brothers and sisters—even if our mother was there all the time. They were spoilt more than I was, better-looking, better pupils and above all, they were never hit. When I heard the muezzin chanting, "Allahu Akbar, Allaaahu... Akbar!" ("God is the greatest") I loved to recite the words after him. My uncle would cry out, "That's a sin! You're chanting the *Azan* (the call to prayer)," and he would smack me. I can't forget it. "Why did you say Murid rather than Uncle Murid?"—"Why did you go to see your Grandfather Abdullah?"—"Why aren't you clearing the table?" They all used to smack me! Including my mother—because I didn't do my chores. And if I didn't like school it was because the teacher also used to smack me. Everyone had the right to hit me, there was no one to say, "Don't do that." The blows could have broken me, but perhaps they made me "too strong-minded."

Because I was being beaten I sometimes went to hide in my maternal grandfather's house, which was only separated from ours by a simple wall. I can remember the smell of Grandfather Abdullah when he took me under his wing and covered me up with a quilt to hide me. My other grandfather, the severe one (but I loved him too), would come looking for me. I would be trembling with fear. He would ask, "Asmaa's not with you is she?" And my other grandfather would reply, "No, she's not here." I could hear his heart beating because I was lying on his chest. When that grandfather died, all my hopes died with him. He relieved me of those fears which, though I was unaware of it at the time, would go with me throughout my life. When I die I want to be buried beside him. He was the only person who treated me with tenderness.

When he stopped being a farmworker he became the imam of a little mosque, a man of religion but kind and peace-loving. He used to listen to Samira Tawfik, a Lebanese singer, "The brown-haired boy is driving me mad...Oh my eyes! He's stolen my spirit, Allah, Allah!" He would listen to that Bedouin song while he was a sheikh, Sheikh Abdullah al-Ghoul. My father and mother are distant cousins—the two branches of the family have the same name. There was no way out for me, I was surrounded by ogres—that's what Al-Ghoul means in Arabic.

3

My Grandfather's Underpants

MY PATERNAL GRANDMOTHER told me that her sister had died in the village in 1948 because someone had dropped a tortoise on her—at that time tortoises were unknown in Palestine. That's not a joke, she literally died of fright. She also told me how extensive their land at Sarafand el-Amar was, the fine vegetables they grew, the paradise it was, how they used to listen to songs and how she'd left the key to the house under the flower-pot and fed the hens so they wouldn't get hungry during the short time she'd be away... and how the family had started to walk, to walk towards Gaza...

Our family's epic journey started in that Palestinian village to the south of Tel Aviv. People said that during the British mandate a British soldier went mad and set fire to it. Once the fire had been extinguished the conurbation had been divided in two: Sarafand el-Kharab (the destroyed) and Sarafand el-Amar (the reconstructed). Whether you come from either of them, the Egyptians, like many Arabs, say that we Palestinians sold our land. But what did we sell? Nothing at all! If we had done so, why on earth would my grandmother have thought she would come back to feed her hens, why would she have put the key under the flower-pot? I feel no attachment to this land that I don't know, but I have loving feelings for my grandmother. She left that place without taking anything with her apart from my grandfather Jomaa's long underpants. He and she took turns wearing them. She told me about it with an embarrassed laugh. "The Jews" (who were not yet Israelis) had simply expelled Palestinian villagers according to a long-established plan, the Plan Dalet. But many, like my grandparents, had fled after having heard that a Jewish squad of the Irgun had massacred two hundred Palestinians in the village of Deir Yassin. They were seized with panic: they were going to be robbed, attacked, assassinated! They said, "Honor (i.e. that of their women) comes before land." That rhymes in Arabic: *"Al 'ard abl el ard."* It's that *'ard,* that "honor," that has always kept us in slavery. Thanks to it (and to the support of the West), Israel occupied our land without meeting any resistance, the Palestinians had fled in order to keep it safe; thanks to it, Hamas got its hands on Gaza by claiming to protect our children from sin, to veil our girls, to forbid them to smoke the hookah in public, to defend their "honor," you understand?

I'm supposed to love the Palestine we have lost, but I refuse to lie and say that I dream of going back to my home country. I regret the loss of that land for my grandmother's sake, but I find it impossible to share her feeling, the compelling desire for a 'return' she's always telling me about. All I know is that you get attached to the place where you've lived and I am very attached to Rafah, the camp where I grew up. In the national tradition of Palestine it is treason to see the camp as a homeland. That means you've given up. As refugees we're supposed to preserve the dream of a return—and in the rhetoric those who were driven out of Palestine call themselves the *A'idun,* the 'returners', that is to say those who will return home. As if the camp were nothing but a transitory reality, an illusion that it would be a crime to cling on to. That is the basis of all our mythology. Since I never knew my family's village, why should I have a 'dream of returning'? And if my refugee camp in the south of the Gaza Strip is like a homeland for me, why should it not be our country? I love Rafah with all my heart, walking along its shores, sitting on its beaches... Even more I love looking at its coast through the window of a car that's moving, because you get greater pleasure from something that doesn't belong to you—like music heard from afar.

I didn't live through the exodus, nor the arrival of my grandparents at Rafah in the flood of refugees. But they've told me about it. They put up their tents, one beside the other on the bare ground, they waited, they despaired, before resigning themselves to building permanent homes. No one drew up a plan, they just went ahead and built their houses with their own hands, one stone on the other, one plank on the other, everybody did the same. After all, they weren't going to bother about aesthetics—it was only a camp!

So I was born in that place where the women slept, while waiting, cold and packed together one beside the other, in those shacks, in that maze of alleyways. We have heard the story so often, the same story in all the families, that I can *see* it as if it were part of my own memories. Our house was made of wood with a corrugated-iron roof and a tiny bathroom, in all it had about ten rooms: there were so many of us! Nine uncles and three aunts, all of them my father's brothers and sisters.

My mother lays me down in a white crib with bars like a prison cell and starts sweeping the house, giving it a thorough wash-down. That is my oldest *real* memory. My father tells me I must have been two and a half, is that possible? He also says, as a joke, "Do you remember those old days? Your mother and I used to do things in front of you, we assumed you wouldn't remember... Do you remember?"

When I was three I started going to the *rawda*, the

nursery school beside the mosque. My father took me there every day. One day I said to him, "I want to go on my own," and he let me do so. I put on my red-checkered apron, the nursery-school uniform, and left. It was quite a long way. Later my father admitted that he'd followed me from a distance—"and I hid when you turned around." That's what Dad was like! He didn't say "no," he let me get on with things but kept a discreet eye on me to be sure nothing would happen to me. It was he who allowed the desire for independence, that I still have today, to blossom.

With the little boys in the *rawda* we would repeat the sexual insults we heard in the streets. But immediately after we would say, "No, no! We want to go to Paradise, not to hell. We're not going to end up in the fire. We must stop talking like that." The nursery school was dependent on UNRWA. We ate their food, it was delicious. Every day we had *muhallabieh*, a chocolate milk-pudding, and I've never eaten such a delicious one since then. UNRWA also gave us very colorful plastic boots which meant that during winter we could walk in the rivulets and on the rutted roads. We were given cod-liver oil, vitamins, coupons for flour, sardines and hummus. My uncles would come for the sacks because they were too heavy for me. We were turned into beggars but I wasn't ashamed: that was our situation.

In the camp the man who sold *barad*, lemon juice mixed with crushed ice with a yellow colorant on the surface, was often to be heard. It was like ice cream, only it wasn't that because milk was rare and expensive. When I smell the aroma of *barad*, or even something that resembles it, the camp and my childhood come back to me at once. Even when there was a curfew, during the occupation, the *barad*-vendor managed to get around the little alleys, out of sight of the army—and did we run to him! They were great times. Back then we didn't think our childhood was happy, but it has become so as it recedes. I've started to miss it. It's strange how memories can transform suffering into happiness. "The past is cloaked in multicolored taffeta and every time we look at it we see a different hue," Milan Kundera said in *Life Is Elsewhere.*

My childhood will forever remain associated with the refugee camp and with my grandfather's house, where my grandmother Zakiyyeh still lived not that long ago. Most of it had been destroyed by the Israeli army during the second Intifada in 2001 but there were two rooms left where she continued to live. Staying for the night with her was a delight, especially when it was raining and the cooing of the pigeons woke me in the morning, as it did when I was a child. Except that the three trees outside the door, a guava, a jasmine and an olive, had disappeared. The Israeli soldiers destroyed the first two and my maternal uncle—may God forgive him—cut down the third. People don't feel anything. The Palestinian refugees' obsession is to have a house, they suffer from permanent insecurity as long as they don't have one. Once they've built it they feel better—in principle. That's why my uncle cut down the olive tree, to put things in order, he said, so that the entrance was clear. He wanted to fit out the house, feel at home and live there with my grandmother. If only he'd stayed there! But he didn't even last six months, he went back to Jordan. He couldn't relax in Gaza, no one can relax in Gaza.

The territory imposes terrible psychological pressure on people. Your family never takes its eyes off you, everyone's talking all the time and interfering in your affairs; if you get married, they want to know when you're going to have your first child, if you give birth they want to know when you'll have your second, if you get a divorce they want to know why and when you're going to get married again. We live under perpetual surveillance, it's very difficult. On the West Bank relationships are more relaxed—perhaps because the space there is less confined. But despite all that, the greater pressure in Gaza makes you feel that people are watching out for you. They miss you if you're away, and you miss them. Abroad no one is really concerned about you nor expresses such warmth toward you. I've been to America, Germany, France, Spain—all well-meaning countries, but they are oozing with indifference. Who knows me over there? Who might harm me? Everything there is normal, everything there is calm. Gaza wounds me and makes me suffer, and yet it is Gaza that draws me to it more and more every day. Foreigners who come to visit us are surprised to see people who are so close, so generous, so loving. But if they have to live there, they have to watch out—the very thing that surrounds you with warmth will eventually suffocate you.

4

The Jews Are Coming

IT WAS IN THE UNITED STATES, when I was twenty-four years old, that I first encountered an Israeli on my own—I mean a civilian. At least that's what I think he was, an Israeli: he was wearing a kippa, perhaps he was just a Jew. I had applied for an internship—open to Palestinian journalists—at the headquarters of the United Nations and by some miracle was among those fortunate enough to be selected. I had never before traveled outside the Arab world and New York left me speechless. A young woman, who had pulled strings to get on the trip, had brought with her all the narrow-mindedness of the people of Gaza. She came out with us, walked around the streets a little and went back to the hotel at six in the evening saying, "My God, New York's not all that different from Gaza."

I would take the subway and head off sometimes without knowing where I was going. I learned to listen to music, to open myself up to art, to meet people... Every day was a breathtaking experience. And all the time I was asking myself, "Am I at peace with myself in a land as free as this, or am I simply a person who limits herself to *talking* about freedom?" I had never before been able to enjoy this freedom, having spent most of my time in Gaza or the United Arab Emirates, but in New York it hit me in the face—and I loved it.

So I met that Israeli (or that Jew) in that city. "Met" is

really an exaggeration, we didn't even speak to each other. All that happened was that we came to the door of a building at the same time, he *opened the door* for me and let me go first with a wave of the hand, and I said, "Thank you." That was all, but that polite gesture, to which I wasn't accustomed, really moved me.

I met another Israeli during the same trip. I was taking part in a session at Colombia University on new media and the Internet, that at that time were not very developed. One of the professors, who was fascinating, had a name that sounded Jewish. Afterwards I went to see him to ask if he was an Israeli. He said yes, but it was only a passport for him, he was a permanently resident in the USA. I said, "This must be the first time an Israeli has taught me something," and he laughed.

I can't think back to my childhood without soldiers: their boots, their weapons, the khaki of their uniforms. Their intrusions, year after year, were so 'normal' in my eyes that my memory can no longer distinguish between them. It was as if we belonged to a society and they to an army of robots coming from outside. I looked on them as inter-changeable characters without individual faces who always played out the same scene, or at least similar scenes that are impossible to arrange in a chronology.

My father came back from the Emirates for short holidays. It's morning, I'm on his knees, my mother has my younger brothers and sisters on hers. We've gathered in our grandparents' room for breakfast with *gharchalleh*—biscuits made in Gaza that you dip into your tea. Grandfather Jomaa is listening to the BBC Arabic service, all his generation were educated by the famous broadcasts: "Here is the BBC London." It's quiet. Suddenly the soldiers attack and we flee, leaving the tea still steaming. What did they want? Nothing special. They come in all the time, just when they feel like it.

We don't even wonder why anymore.

My father's in Gaza once more. We're woken at dawn by terrible thumps on the door—the soldiers! But this time it's the front door. From the window my father sees one of them banging his head against a wall on which is written, "You're treating us they way the Nazis treated you." They've cordoned off the whole of Block O in order to find the one who wrote the graffiti, they make the people come out, pushing and shoving them. They drag my grandfather out, still in his pajamas. He's old, it's cold. They shout at him in Arabic, "Your children wrote these slogans, you have to rub them out," and hit him in front of us. My grandfather complies, a soldier at his back. They have nothing against him in particular, they make all the old men do this—because the younger ones have managed to slip away.

Another image: I'm hiding under the table in the dining room. I see the soldiers' legs passing to and fro, I know they're looking for my uncles. One of them hears me, he suddenly bends down. He's disappointed when he sees it's only a little girl, and he slaps me.

It's summer. I'm playing out in the street behind my uncle's truck. The soldiers come past, one of them offers me a sweet. I refuse it. He asks, "Why?" He speaks in Arabic, he's a Druze.[1]

"Because there's poison in it." I can't believe it's a real sweet, impossible. Through the violence, this kind of thing has imprinted itself on our children's minds.

There are many Druzes in the Israeli army. I see them on my way to the *rawda*, they sometimes touch themselves and make obscene gestures as we pass, they say "daughters of whores," things like that.

1 The Druzes are a mountain people spread over Lebanon, Syria and Israel. Heterodox Muslims, their doctrine purports to be a synthesis of Muslim mysticism and Persian and Indian religions. The Israeli Druzes do their military service in the Israeli army.

It's the Intifada. The Israeli army starts using sharpened stones to bombard us, it's like sending a lot of knives that land on the zinc roofs, transforming them at one blow into a sieves, into tin lace. As soon as we hear the explosions we run to hide in the only place where the roof is solid, the bathroom. The stones fall down like a heavy shower of rain.

The doors of our house are open, people are running over to take shelter. The soldiers are throwing black leather grenades that give off a special tear-gas. One of these grenades lands at my feet, I bend down over it, I become unconscious. My uncles run over and throw water on my face. I come to again. To combat the tear-gas we have onions, *nashader*—a kind of chemical salt that wakes you up—and a widespread eau de cologne called 55 555, five times five. We offer the whole range to those who've taken refuge in our house. When they've been hit by rubber bullets we bandage them. But it's more complicated when it's real bullets. Most often they die.

I know all the little alleyways that allow me to avoid the soldiers when I'm going to school. Every morning I say to myself, "May God protect us, let's hope nothing happens." But on this day they launch a surprise attack. I'm so terrified that I run to hide in our neighbors' chicken coop; other girls join me. We look out through the fine mesh, we're trembling, the bursts of machine-gun fire resound inside our skulls.

We're at school, we hear vehicles screaming to a halt, the cavalcade of the soldiers cordoning off the district, then shots. We're crying, we gather around the teacher... She's distraught, she feels responsible for the children, the soldiers are everywhere. She tells us to stay in the yard but we're not listening to her, we go out into the street, crying with fear. I take off, I see people lying on the ground injured, I think it's the end, I'm going to die. I look for somewhere to hide, but it's difficult: the whole village has closed up in a flash. I come across another school, it's the first time in my life I've seen it. I go in, I look around—I don't know anyone there. I start to recite the verses of the Koran I know by heart, for a long time, until the soldiers go away. Once back home I find my parents going out of their minds with anxiety. For them I'd disappeared.

The soldiers attack our house. My father and my uncles have time to run off and hide in my other grandfather's house that adjoins ours. And we, the girls and the women, including my two grandmothers, stay locked in the little bathroom with the solid roof. In that tiny space we're shouting, we're crying, it's all the more oppressive because we're in the middle of the Ramadan fast, we're dying of thirst. We can hear the cries of my uncles in the other house next door. My mother's worried, she gets up on a stool to look out of the bathroom window. She's horrified at what she sees: my grandfather's ground is covered in trails of blood! We cry even more but the soldiers don't come to see what's happening. They mean no harm to the women, they're only interested in the men. They stay in our house, hoping the fugitives who've escaped them will come back. When they finally leave, we run over to the house next door. My uncle Murid, his head split open, is crying all the time, "I want to die a martyr!" We put him in a car and send him to the hospital. My father is also wounded but it's not too serious. He tells us what happened. When they launched the attack, the soldiers found my uncles and started to beat them up. But some of our neighbors surrounded the house and started throwing stones at them. Several soldiers were wounded. Some took the clothes that were hanging out on the lines to dry in order to wipe off the blood—that's the blood my mother saw from the window. The soldiers were trapped. Some others came and managed to get them out. They went, leaving my uncles on the ground, covered in blood. We really thought Uncle

Murid was going to die. It was a terrible day, and also the day on which my uncles became famous: the implication of the attack by the Israeli army was that they were important militants. From that time on, a bearded sheikh regularly came on his bicycle to bring us some yoghurt and some bread: a gift from Hamas to its members.

5

Your Dolls Have a Soul

THE SOLDIERS terrified me more than my uncles did, but I didn't have to live with them all day, every day. My childhood was unhappy because of the Israelis but even more so because of my uncles, who used to hit me. On the other hand, I was afraid of losing my uncles because I loved them. How could I find myself in this tangle of emotions?

Hamas was popular at that time. They had won people's hearts because their first communiqués were remarkable: beautiful Arabic, verses of poetry, lines from the Koran... They were very good at communication. For example, they put on plays inside the mosques for an exclusively female audience. On the improvised stage women and girls played both male and female roles, including those of Israeli soldiers. My aunt played a woman militant whom the soldiers were trying to persuade to become a collaborator. She resisted as well as she could and in the end she died. I started crying there in the mosque, shouting, "My aunt, my aunt!" No one could make me stop. She had to get up herself and come and show me she was still alive. Can you imagine women in a mosque acting a play put on by Hamas? You wouldn't see something like that today! Back then they showed intelligence. Compared with them Fatah, founded by Yasser Arafat, cut a sorry figure: it was no use them being the historical institution that had unified the Palestinians, allowing them to exist in the eyes of the world; their propaganda was repetitive and completely lacking in imagination. In the conflict that pitted the Israeli army against Hamas, Fatah looked more and more to be on the sidelines. But people were divided by the introduction of religious ideas in what was called the 'spirit of resistance'. From that point on there were the 'true Muslims' and the others who were soon engaged in a conflict that threatened to become bloody.

One day our house was attacked by some young people whose long hair indicated that they belonged to the Popular Front—one of the oldest left-wing secular organizations of the Palestinian movement. Armed with chains and Molotov cocktails they came at the house yelling that they were going to kill my uncles. Terrified, all I said to myself was, "It's a good thing Papa's away." They tried to jump over the iron gate to the house and I remembered having seen them a few months previously with my uncles—they were friends! But things had changed. Now I could *feel* that they were assassins; until then I'd never had that feeling about anyone else. Fortunately people intervened and stopped them. They then said that they had come to avenge one of their comrades killed by Hamas and that the victim's mother had cursed our family—he was her only son. At the far end of our district an old woman had a little candy store where I used to go to buy chewing gum, candy and chocolate of a kind I've never seen since. I believe that woman was the mother in question, though I'm not absolutely sure. The affair was eventually sorted out and I went back to the woman's shop and she, for her part, continued to sell me her candy as if nothing had happened.

The portraits of the 'martyrs' posted on the walls of the camp had become rarer because at that time Hamas had forbidden the representation of the human face. My father, who was good at drawing, did a certain number. Unlike his brothers, he didn't belong to Hamas nor to any other organization and limited himself to drawing for anyone who asked him to. The reduction in commissions was a kind of measure of the progress of the religious outlook. We also felt it at home. As soon as they joined Hamas, my uncles stopped laughing, even smiling. Uncle Saïd started heaping reproaches on his sisters who went to the university: "How did you get back? Who was with you?" I had some Barbie dolls, not genuine ones, of course, there were no Barbie dolls in Gaza, but cheap rag copies sold from a blanket on the ground outside the dispensary. Sometimes we were given them when there were parties—Grandfather Abdullah loved to give me presents. My Uncle Saïd, who was very pious, told me, "Your dolls have a soul, it's sinful." That made a great impression on me. The idea that the doll I had in my hands had a soul was a little frightening... So I tore them all up into pieces, even though no one had told me to. Grandfather Abdullah was annoyed. "You're wrong. What do your dolls have to do with religion?" Having thought I'd done a good deed, I now regretted having destroyed my dolls, but it was too late.

That same year my mother gave birth to my brother Abdullah. I was outside when I heard the news. I ran through the alleyways in the camp to get home as quickly as possible, cutting across a really filthy district where there was a family who relieved themselves out in the street. I slipped and fell in some shit, dirtying my clothes and hands. I hurried to my grandfather's where I gave myself a good wash with soap and water; my grandmother bawled me out because I hadn't been careful. Even after that, it still smelt of shit whenever I sniffed. When I set off again my enthusiasm had gone. I was wary now and kept looking this way and that. Once more I had destroyed my joy.

Then my father wrote to tell us we were to go and join

him: we were all going to live together in the Emirates. That was in 1990. I realized I was going to be away for a long time from the house in Rafah, where my uncles lived and my mother had to suffer the daily criticism from my father's family. However, at the moment we left, we all burst into tears. I felt immensely sad, we all embraced each other... I never imagined a separation could be so heartrending. The big taxi arrived, we stowed our luggage and got in, my mother and the six of us. The previous evening I'd gone to the trouble of cutting up a pack of cards in small pieces. When the taxi drove off I scattered those little bits of cardboard over my uncles, my aunts, all the inhabitants of the house. It was my way of saying goodbye.

Abdullah was the last of the six children to have lived in Gaza during the Intifada. The three others were born later, in the Emirates. We have the children of the Intifada and the children of the Gulf: they have nothing to do with each other.

6

The Sufferings of the Grave

ONE OF OUR TEACHERS at school was Egyptian. When she suggested we buy audio cassettes with stories recorded on them, it was too expensive for us. My father recorded a story himself, in his own voice. During the recording my little brother Abdullah starting crying and while we were listening to the recording during a lesson and heard my brother's voice, everyone began to make fun of me. But the teacher said, "Stop it! Asmaa made it herself, it's brilliant."

Our English teacher was Tunisian, an unmarried woman who was so nice we all became very good at English. To an inspector who was questioning me I said, without thinking, that Tunisians didn't fast during Ramadan. The teacher said, "But how do you know?" There was one Tunisian in the class, a girl called Sayda who was annoyed. "It's true we don't cover our heads," she said, "but we do fast and pray."

I replied, "I fast during Ramadan too, and I get along very well with God, I always say to Him, 'Good night, God,' before going to sleep." Sayda became my friend.

Our Arabic teacher was from the Emirates. Once I handed in my work a day late. For me it was a creation several pages long; for her it was just a piece of homework, and she refused to accept it. Fortunately my father read it and liked it very much. But I liked our Arabic teacher despite that. She wore a veil and confessed that she had problems with the other sects, the Alouites and the Shiites... It was the first time I had heard those words, Alouites, Shiites, and I didn't understand. I asked myself, "What's she talking about? Is she talking about the Jews?"

Our drawing teacher was also Egyptian, she was quite old and wore a kind of coif decorated with pearls. I had drawn a heart I was quite pleased with and gave it to her. She looked at it and smacked me. "Badly brought-up little girl! A heart, love—nothing but empty words!" She told me to erase it. That made me very sad, for I really loved drawing.

Hundreds of thousands of Egyptians, Syrians, Iraqis, Palestinians, and Lebanese worked in the Emirates or the other Gulf states, and not only in education. Entrepreneurs, businessmen, doctors, craftsmen, laborers—they came from all over the world to earn their living or to try and make a fortune in the land of black gold. During the years they spent there, many adopted the local customs, made their wives wear veils, went to the mosque more often than they used to and became accustomed to their role as dominant male in the family. The superstitious and retrograde climate they were immersed in was illustrated by stories of "sufferings of the grave" such as we were told at school: after death, God was going to punish us if we behaved badly. "They opened the grave of a woman who wore short skirts while she was alive," it said in one of those stories, "and they found that her legs had been burnt..." A woman preacher who came to talk to us about religious practices also concentrated on the "sufferings of the grave"—it was the standard term—and assured us that we would go to hell if we liked musicians and singers.

Of course, I didn't believe a word of this, but these were lessons that were meant to terrify us. All we heard was people talking about a terrible God with a stick to punish us.

Naturally once the Arab expatriates returned home they would spread this obscurantist model. That is the secret of the almost mechanical spread of hard-line Islam that was a breeding ground for Islamism, not to mention the multitude of koranic schools financed by the Gulf states. Fortunately I had my father to offset this. He would tell us marvelous stories about God, he would make us laugh, he didn't force anything on us. "God isn't the way they say," he told us, "He is the Merciful, the Compassionate. A person who gives up their heart to God is a Muslim, whatever their religion."

I was poor at school; the pupils giggled because I wrote "Falastine" with the letter 'sād' instead of 'sīn'. The girls all cried out, "A Palestinian who doesn't know how to spell her country's name!" and they laughed. I was ashamed. I was used to not doing very well at school in Gaza, but not to that extent! I had so many brothers and sisters and our house was so poorly furnished that I didn't invite my classmates to visit me. The day when, at school, I was given some clothes and a new schoolbag, I was very pleased and when I got home I said, "Look what the teacher gave me!" Papa and Mama said, "Very nice," but exchanged a look. It was only later that I realized they were gifts as part of an aid program for poor girls.

In that melting pot of the Arab world that was the Emirates I had the feeling that I represented 'the Palestinian girl'—in the 'refugee' version. Every time I asked for something, my father would say, "Listen, I'd have to buy six of what you're asking for, one for each of your brothers and sisters." His work wasn't going very well; there were few requests for architectural drawings. We were living in Al-Aïn, a village in the interior 170 kilometers from Abu Dhabi. While we were waiting for things to sort themselves out, we were living with relatives of another branch of the family who lived in an apartment block. It had been decided to split their apartment in two. Since they were better off than us—the head of the family was a businessman—they had air conditioning in their part, while we in ours suffered from temperatures that could rise over 120 degrees, like being in a furnace.

Reading was my only outlet. In Gaza I'd discovered my father's hidden library and started to read. It wasn't really secret, the books had just been thrown into a room full of junk and remained there. My father read a lot; most of them were works on Islam. There was also an Arabic translation of the famous *The Outsider* by Colin Wilson, who talked about Camus, Sartre, Hemingway, Dostoyevsky, Nijinsky, van Gogh and others. In the Emirates I discovered that my father had other, far better books: works by Nagib Mahfouz, Ihsan Abdel Quddous or Fathi Yaken. I set about reading everything. I was hopeless at school, no good at spelling, but I devoured books.

One day at school we were summoned to a routine eye test. The doctor said to me, "Look here, look there," and he discovered that I could only see with one eye. I was vaguely aware of that but thought it was the same for everyone; when I was small in the camp, I kept on falling all the time—I walked and I fell. Grandfather Abdullah had taken me to the UNWRA doctor. But the doctor was an idiot. "There's nothing wrong with her," he concluded. With thousands of refugees to look after he wasn't going to bother with a little girl of four whose grandfather said, "She falls a lot." Grandfather came back from the consultation complaining about the doctor, shaking his head and muttering, "That's not possible," while he was nothing but a simple imam.

If they had followed his intuition and diagnosed the problem, they could have treated my eye. But after the age of six, what is called a *lazy eye* cannot be saved: the optic nerve is dead. When my parents heard that they went wild. My father took me to different doctors, in particular to an Indian eye specialist who was visiting Abu Dhabi. We went there on the bus because a taxi was too expensive, taking sandwiches to eat on the journey. The doctor gave me some exercises to do, he told me to put a blindfold over my good eye for two hours a day. He imagined that would reinforce the other eye. I wailed and cried because I could no longer see anything. How could I walk? The doctor knew there was no hope, but he tried. I would move the blindfold a little so I could see out under it. He'd also made me wear glasses that I kept on losing. I spent my time looking for them; I would find them under the settees. All the doctors we consulted after that told us the same thing: I should have been treated sooner.

During all this agitation we heard some terrible news: my Grandfather Abdullah, whom I loved so much, had died of stomach cancer. We called Gaza, called ceaselessly, I spent four days on the telephone crying, we couldn't go for the funeral, our eyes were swollen with tears. My mother fell ill, my father did the cooking. He was very loving, he took account of everyone's feelings. When my mother got up, she saw we were crying, me in particular, and my father, impassive, continued to feed and look after us.

If my Grandfather Jomaa had taught me tolerance toward other peoples, Grandfather Abdullah had taught me religious tolerance. We said goodbye to him as well as we could in that house, then we moved.

7

Saved by Books

IN OUR NEW HOUSE, I found that my father had had a room built for me alone. In principle that's not allowed in a rented property, but we were on the ground floor and there was an internal courtyard that wasn't used at all. He'd made it without asking anyone so that I could keep my books and magazines there and above all to allow me to read and write in peace—the rest of the house being somewhat overcrowded. In that room, the first that was truly my own, I met lots of fascinating people—in books, I mean. I went to school and came home as quickly as I could in order to get back to them. At the beginning I wasn't there in anyone's real life, being too preoccupied with my reading. Where we were now there were a lot more Palestinian pupils, while Egyptians and girls from the Gulf had been in the majority at my previous school. My results quickly improved.

"Mummy, look at the grade I got in Spelling!"

She went on hanging out the washing without turning around. "Zero, as usual..."

"Of course not! 9.5 out of ten!"

I soon started to have friends, girls who lived nearby and approached me. I was almost becoming popular. In the town there was a garden reserved for women, Al Jahili Park, and I joined a number of girls who used to meet there. We would go there on Thursdays, sometimes on a Monday. I would take books with me, detective stories or romantic novels I'd found in my father's library. The girls would crowd around me. While I was reading out loud they would forget my material poverty, my clothes that came from refugee aid, my poor grades at school... Thanks to literature I was no longer a Palestinian refugee. The girls would phone me all the time, insisting I come over and read them some stories or listen to them telling me about their problems. Now I had a face and a first name.

Nothing suited my mother, neither the fact that I had friends, nor that I went to the park, nor above all that I rode the bicycle a boy who lived nearby lent me. I no longer listened to her. Every day I refused more and more to let her forbid me anything. I didn't listen to her any longer. What I didn't realize was that I was becoming an adolescent. My mother couldn't quite understand what was happening to me. My father could, but he let me do as I liked. It was in the Al-Jahili Park that I had my first period. I ran home to tell my mother—she hadn't warned me at all. Fortunately my friends had explained it all to me already so that I wasn't frightened by it. One night my father woke up to find me watching a video cassette with a couple kissing. It was *Hero*, a film with Dustin Hoffman. I felt ashamed but my father said nothing. He just went back to bed. My mother tried to talk to me the next day without really getting around to it. What could she say? I already knew more than she did.

When my father gave me a scarf I was angry with him. His present implied that I should cover my hair because of puberty but I refused to accept that. I wrote him a letter to indicate my refusal and I stopped talking to him. After a while he came to tell me, "It's over, let's forget it. You aren't obliged to cover your head." I did, however, start half-wearing the scarf, letting my hair show. All the girls did the same, at least those whose parents were like mine.

The neighbors' son was called Ali, his sisters were friends of mine. The two of us were around thirteen or fourteen and we had exchanged pledges: two half-moons worn on a fine chain around the neck. Mine said, "There is no other god but God," his, "And Mohammed is the prophet of God." I would go to visit my friends, his sisters, and we would end up sitting in the same parlor, he and I. We never spoke to each other in front of the others, even his sisters didn't notice anything. We would look at each other from afar. It was a childish thing. We never kissed, didn't even hold each other's hand—nevertheless we were the children of two Palestinian refugee families from Rafah Camp. The only thing was that we spoke to each other at night, from window to window. We told each other that we were going to go out together without our parents knowing anything about it. In the end we never did that. My father caught me talking to him from the window. He remained silent for a moment, then said, "He's not suitable for you, that boy, you're much more intelligent than he is." He didn't say, "What?! You're talking to a boy in the middle of the night!" He neither insulted me nor reproached me at all, he just made me think that the boy was a bit stupid. I gave him back the chain... My father always had a great influence on me. I thought about the fact that in my fledgling love life I had let him have the last word. I thought about the Electra complex... then I put it out of my mind.

At school the girls were attracted to each other, they sent secret letters to each other. "Why shouldn't I do the same as them," I wondered. I had noticed a very pretty girl, she came from the Emirates and was called Meissa. It was like something out of a story: she was the princess of the place and we, the little strangers, bowed in admiration before her. I sent her a letter and she replied at once. We started to go to the women's garden together, we talked, we told each other everything. She wasn't highly intelligent but very nice. We told each other stories about girls, what this one did, what happened to that one; we behaved exactly as if we were in love with each other when we weren't. Two girls had been caught together in the school washroom. That is widespread in the Gulf because there is no natural relationship between men and women.

But that wasn't my priority. I was already writing poems, one of them talked about a cascade and a white moon, when I'd never seen a cascade anymore than a white moon—it's not in the Emirates that you could find something like that. The rhythm of my writing was accelerating: poems, novellas, stories. I wrote anywhere—at home, at school, in the garden— in a notebook that I kept with me all the time. At home I would read what I'd written to my father. I also started to keep a diary in which I wrote down everything that happened to me and admitted my secret admiration for writers and artists.

8

The Valley of Flowers

IN THE EMIRATES, Palestine never let go of us. When the first Gulf War broke out in 1990, Yasser Arafat declared himself in favor of Saddam Hussein, who had just invaded Kuwait. That gesture provoked the anger of the Emirati authorities toward the Palestinians. In reprisal we were no longer allowed to attend the free public school. And the private schools were very expensive. My father had already lost his job as a municipal engineer because he had accepted work from outside—doing architectural drawings at home. Someone had reported him out of pure spite. But now, on top of the rent and everyday expenses he had to pay for the schooling of six children. When he eventually managed to find another, better-paid job it was in Abu Dhabi, two hours away from where we lived. He spent five days of the week there, only coming back to Al Aïn at the weekend. When I was on holiday I was sometimes allowed to go with him.

The Intifada, the 'revolt of stones' launched in 1987 and popularized throughout the world because of its quasi non-violent nature, also made us live with an awareness of our identity as Palestinians. We gathered around the TV in the evening to follow its twists and turns—and I in the secret hope of seeing our house in Rafah. On the day in 1993 when this uprising led to the signing of the Oslo Accords that foresaw a negotiated resolution of the Israeli-Palestinian conflict, none of us could believe our eyes. It took the sight on the TV of Yasser Arafat entering Gaza in July 1994, acclaimed by a jubilant crowd, to convince us. There was no doubt anymore: the old Palestinian leader had also succeeded in 'liberating Jerusalem.' Our joy was only intensified by our previous incredulity. Overwhelmed, we literally started jumping up and down before going out to proclaim our joy in the streets of Al Aïn. Almost the whole female population of the town met in Al Jahili Park, hugging and kissing and crying out in jubilation. When we got back home, the scene of Arafat in Gaza was run again and again on the TV. We couldn't see it often enough.

Later that evening, some hooded Hamas militants appeared on the screen vehemently denouncing the Oslo Accords that had allowed Arafat to return. In our euphoria we looked on them as killjoys, bad losers. It was too early to foresee that the course of events would unfortunately prove them right: the assassination of Rabin, the Israeli prime minister, would call everything into question, Arafat had not liberated anything at all, the concessions he had made were not going to lead anywhere, the Oslo Accords were to lead to an impasse and terrible divisions... But for the time being our hope was still alive: we so longed to see the problem resolved once and for all.

There was something else happening at the same time. A few months earlier my father had heard during a telephone call to Gaza that my Uncle Saïd, wanted by the Israeli army for his military activity in Rafah, had been wounded by bullets when he was arrested. His wound hadn't been dressed in prison, or had been badly dressed, that wasn't clear. Another prisoner said that he'd seen worms coming out of the wound; he'd almost lost his leg but had finally been saved at the last minute. After a long time behind bars, he had been one of a group of 417 leaders and officials of Hamas and the Islamic Jihad whom the Israeli authorities held isolated in a little hamlet, Marj el Zuhour (the Valley of Flowers), at the southern extremity of Lebanon, which they were occupying. There the prisoners had taken advantage of the situation to pursue a very effective propaganda campaign for their ideas. Uncle Saïd managed, if only rarely, to telephone us from his exile. His sister, my aunt, was studying pharmacy in the Yemen and my father started sending her money so that she could finish her course.

When I saw him again years later my uncle told me he had very happy memories of his exile in southern Lebanon. He'd managed to buy a horse there; he and his comrades used to melt the snow to make tea; the Lebanese Shiite farmers came to visit them and relationships among the 417 exiles became particularly close. When he came back to Gaza, Yasser Arafat's Palestinian Authority was already in place, and it was particularly suspicious of the leaders and officials of Hamas who had been released—in fact they were promptly put in prison, which my Uncle Saïd wanted to avoid at all cost; he'd had enough of it. Therefore when he came back from exile he moved away from the Islamist movement to become an English teacher employed by the national Ministry of Education of the Palestinian Authority. He found his beloved wife Nistrine again, and they had three girls and one boy. He seemed to have come to understand the meaning of life and its beauty. But in 2007, when Hamas took over power in the territory, he gave up teaching to take his place in the security service of the Islamist movement.

Most of the new leaders in Gaza, who are still in power today, were his comrades, the former detainees of Marj el Zuhour.

9

Something That Doesn't Take Root

THE EMIRATI COMPANY where my father worked started paying his salary late. Suddenly it owed him a lot of money: 40,000 dirhams, about $13,200. He could no longer pay the bills. The electricity company cut off the power at the moment when the temperature was approaching 120 degrees. To escape the heat, we got into the habit of spending the night under the trees in a nearby garden. And when we slept at home, we left all the doors open. One night, I opened my eyes to see burglars in the room, at the foot of my bed! I cried out loud before fainting. When I came to again the police were in the apartment.

The situation didn't change however—we were still without electricity. But my father was not the kind of man to give up easily, he was a fighter. He gathered us all together— there were nine of us children by then—and explained that we were going to sleep on the premises of the Abu Dhabi firm where he worked. It was the first time in my life that I took part in an occupation!

We went there, opened the doors and put down our bundles. The bosses were dumbfounded. They didn't expect to see a family of Palestinian refugees coming to camp in their offices. If they were refusing to pay my father, it was out of nastiness and pure avarice. And also out of contempt. They drove around in their Mercedes and lived in sumptuous villas, without a thought for the poor little Palestinian engineer who had his family to support. I slept under the big table in the committee room. My father brought provisions and we ate at the same table. There was air conditioning and we went to the nearby beach every day—it had become our home! The boss came from time to time for a quick, flurried glance, but that didn't bother us at all. Or mostly not... On some mornings it wasn't that easy to wake up surrounded by employees arriving for work. But my father was obstinate, and I respected his obstinacy. He was within his rights and was teaching me to be proud of what we were doing. If he had taken no action, simply groaned and gotten into debt, I would never have become what I am today. Sometimes strength springs from humiliation as long as you refuse to accept it, face up to it. We camped out in the offices for a week, and what a week that was! A great time! Despite the poverty and the problems, we were happy. I woke up in the middle of the night and saw Papa and Mama kissing.

The bosses eventually gave way. They paid the whole of the withheld salary in order to see us leave. We were so pleased we threw all those hard-earned banknotes up in the air. My father announced, "We're going back to Gaza." I was delighted: the previous year we'd gone back for a short visit and I'd fallen in love with a cousin who had come back from Libya. My mother wasn't very happy with the idea. She didn't want to go back to my Grandfather Jomaa, fearing she'd be subjected to criticism again. My father reassured her. "I've been sending off money each month to build a new house in Rafah," he said. "It's not finished yet but it already looks fine, we'll live in it." We said goodbye to our friends, the girls gave a little farewell party for me in Al Jahili Gardens, the neighbors cried. We left swearing never to come back again.

The Gulf is a strange world, pretty unreal. Nature does not exist in those countries, there are just houses piled up one against the other. If you wanted to see the desert you had to go on an excursion. My father would lead all six of us (the other three were babies) in single file like ducklings, along the side of the road. We walked like that as far as the border with Oman, we followed our father because we loved him so. All the same, we said to him, "We can't go any farther, Papa, we're too tired."

"It won't be long now, we're almost there."

He was lying, we still had a long way to go. We sat down in parks, unwrapped Laughing Cow cheeses that we ate out in the open, what wonderful souvenirs! Our father never made us feel we were poor. We arrived, exhausted and starving, in Bremi, the nearest town to Al Aïn, where we had some *handal* to eat, a kind of little watermelon that was acid and bitter. In the Emirates we never ate at McDonald's or Hardy's—as my uncle and his daughter did—it was too expensive. But we had two video cassette players at home and my father showed us the best films in the world, dramas, adventures, horror films, action movies—which my cousin never got to see. Freedom of thought, the cinema, music, reading, that's what made us what we are. Almost all the members of my family—apart from one brother and one sister who studied medicine and ophthalmology—have tended toward artistic fields—painting, film, literature—because our father had accustomed us to that since we were little.

I understand everything that gets written about the Emirates because I know how people think in that society that believes it is religious but isn't. What does the religious power want basically? That Gaza should become a society in the image of the Gulf. That boys and girls should be separated in all places, that girls shouldn't smoke the hookah, that women should be veiled and subject to their husbands, that the avenues should be nice and clean, that the trees should be cut down to widen the streets. All of that has absolutely no connection with religion. Those are hidebound, corrupt societies, covered in mosques where children are oppressed by being compelled to study the Koran.

The Emirates can have an influence on you but can't educate you, there is something there that doesn't take root. The country didn't give me the capacity to say, "This is what I reject, that is what I want." For example, when my father gave me the scarf to cover my hair, I half went along with it. It's Gaza that turned me into a rebel.

10

By the Sea

I WAS EIGHT when I went to the Emirates, sixteen when I came back. I was perhaps under the illusion that I could take up my previous life again but now I was a young woman—and Gaza had become stricter. It was 1998. I started going out with my head half-covered and talking to my male cousins, and it wasn't long before people were speaking ill of me. They would shout as I went past, "It's the girl who's come from abroad and dresses in that indecent manner." I went to the beach with my brothers, which wasn't done: the seashore has a very bad reputation, it's looked on as a place where bad things go on: sex, hashish, debauchery. When people say about a young woman that her boyfriend 'took her to the beach' the suggestion is that they behaved badly. My uncles phoned my father, who had stayed in the Emirates to settle his affairs:

"Your daughter went to the beach, God knows what happened."

"What are you insinuating? If you have something to say to her, say it to her face."

They had a go at that, Uncle Fahdi and Uncle Saïd, each in his turn. I replied calmly, "I've done nothing wrong, there's no risk. I know myself, I'm my own keeper."

They didn't know what to say to that. It wasn't the first time they'd called my father to complain about the way I dressed or behaved. They also intervened every time I had a new girlfriend, saying things like, "That girl's not right, her mother has a very bad reputation..."

I had just met a great girl, Imane, who claimed to be an atheist. She belonged to one of the Palestinian families which had been expelled from Egypt and lived in a camp people called Canada. People looked askance at her because she wore trousers and did as she saw fit—it was natural that we should understand each other. We spent most of our time together, sometimes at my place, sometimes at hers, but every day. We bought potato chips and chocolate and talked for hours on end. She had her own particular way of thinking. One day when we were out in street I said to her, "Have you seen the way people are looking at that couple in front of us? It's intolerable!"

"Yes, but we're looking at them as well. Whatever we may say, we're still children of this environment and of this outlook, our eyes are attracted in the same way to anything out of the ordinary. We don't just have to change the way people look at things but the way we look too."

I understood how she used her brain. I said nothing. She was going to remain my friend for a long time. Imane was not the only one who helped me find where I belonged in Rafah. There was also one of my mother's brothers, Uncle Ahmed, a poet with a degree in Arabic literature. He had a fine library which he'd brought back in cardboard boxes from Libya, where he'd been working. I discovered the writer Ghada al-Samman, the former mistress of the famous Palestinian writer Ghassan Khanafani. Theirs was a particularly tumultuous relationship. She regularly rebuffed him and spoke about their love with a strength and freedom that impressed me. Even though that had happened in the 1970s, a more liberal time than ours, the mere fact that this passion could exist in the Arab and Palestinian world gave me courage. I started reading anything I could lay my hands on by Ghada al-Samman, in particular her *Unfinished Works*. In my Uncle Ahmed's library I also discovered Tolstoy's *War and Peace*, Nabokov's *Lolita* and Dostoyevsky, Shakespeare, Tagore, Rimbaud, all the great books... The experience of real writing made me tremble. I wondered whether I wanted to be a novelist rather than a poet—but did I have the ability? I took the books one after the other and returned them when I'd finished reading them. If I didn't, then I was in trouble with my uncle. We would discuss philosophy and literature together. He sometimes got fed up with me because I talked too much. His library was burnt in the course of the Israeli invasion of 2001 during the second Intifada. I walked among charred books. My uncle cried over his lost library. All we managed to save were three books on psychology.

He never asked me embarrassing questions, he never poked his nose in my affairs. As we were going into the school one day Saleh, the English teacher I was in love with, slipped a poem in my hand that described love as a *Karbala*. I didn't know what the word meant so I showed the poem to Uncle Ahmed. He didn't ask who this teacher was who wrote verses for me, he simply explained as best he could, "Every year the Shiites celebrate the martyrdom of Hussain, the grandson of the Prophet who was killed at Karbala, by beating themselves until they bleed." So the poem evoked this bloody celebration as a comparison with the sufferings of love you impose on yourself. I was impressed—but I can't say I found the comparison very sexy.

Well before Saleh gave me this poem, I had written one for him, phrased in such a way that no one would suspect who it was addressed to. I faxed it to *Al Ayyam* (The Days), a well-known newspaper from Ramallah. To be published was a dream come true in the refugee camp. A few days later, *Al Ayyam* had my poem in its cultural supplement *Yaraat*

(Little Butterflies)—and I was only sixteen! The next day someone was hammering at my door. It was Uncle Fahdi, with the paper in his hand. "How could you do that? Are you out of your mind? Never in our family has a young girl published a love poem!" And there I was, thinking they'd be proud of me. Fortunately my father and my mother were, and even prouder than I could have hoped. For them, the important thing was that a big newspaper had published me.

Uncle Fahdi said to me, "Come on, we're going to have a talk." He wanted to drive me to the beach. While he was looking for his keys, my mother started hopping up and down and screaming. "He's going to kill you and throw you in the sea!"—thinking the beach could also be a crime scene. But I replied, "No, I'm sure he won't do anything, we're just going to talk."

And that's what happened. We walked along the beach, and I was expecting him to attack me because of the poem. Instead he asked, "Do you belong to the Popular Front?"

"No, not at all."

"But all your friends are left-wingers, all those girls are in it."

I understood his problem. I'd just written a play that an amateur theater group was going to put on. They didn't have a place where they could rehearse, so I'd invited them into our house. The neighbors went wild—how could I have young people of both sexes acting out scenes in our home? My uncle tried to talk to me about my behavior in general, making a connection between the poem I sent to *Al Ayyam* and the play I was involved in putting on. I kept a low profile. "My friends may be members of the Popular Front, but I'm not."

We continued talking as we walked along the beach. All he could do was to repeat the standard arguments. "Those people in the Popular Front are lost, we are the ones who will go to Paradise, not them. We are Islam, and we have to serve Islam. Our thoughts and our pens must contribute to that."

"But how do you know I don't serve Islam in my own way?"

He had no idea what to say. He didn't read, nor had any ideas of his own about things. All he could do was to say what is allowed and what is a sin. For lack of arguments, there was nothing left for him but to take me back home, to the great relief of my mother.

The play was eventually put on. It was a succession of short scenes talking about childhood. One was set among the family, another out in the street, the third at school. *Our Lost Childhood*—that was its title—was such a success that it was awarded the first prize in a competition. When the result was announced my father and my mother, who were in the theater, jumped up, shouting for joy; one of my brothers and one of my sisters were acting in the play. The whole family, who had rejected the theater and had argued against me fiercely, were in that very theater, weeping tears of pride— except for my uncles, who had refused to attend the show, continuing to say, "You are unbelievers, you're destroying the world." The times when Hamas put on plays in the mosques were definitely over.

11

The Temptation of the Veil

MY FRIEND Imane was angry with me and I with her. It's not the first time. We've been arguing a lot recently because of jealous girls, of my uncles who made her feel she wasn't welcome, of stupid things. But this time I felt, without knowing why, that it was more serious. I took refuge up on the roof and wrote a short story for her, *You and Me*. You would say it was a declaration of love to a boy, there's nothing to indicate I was talking to a girl. I sent it to her, nothing happened. I waited one day, then a second... I went back up on the roof, I stayed there, I didn't feel like going down again. Without Imane I had the feeling I was alone in a nasty world. It wasn't just the problem of the East. I thought of Kundera again who also describes closed societies which repress beauty in all its forms, beauty of the body, of the soul, of art, because they simply can't understand it. I was having to cope with a world like that and no longer had anyone to help me.

My whole life I've never had time to be happy, everything inside me is mobilized in order to keep me standing up straight and advancing. Even in love, it wasn't happiness I was seeking but the ability to stand firm, to keep on loving. And suddenly a feeling of discouragement I'd never known before took hold of me. It wasn't just about Imane. The pressures I'd been using all my strength to resist since I came back from the Emirates—hostile looks, hurtful comments, muttered slander, mute disapproval, scarcely concealed hostility—suddenly became a heavy burden. It was physical. My body could no longer sustain the state of tension I'd been living in day after day. Something had collapsed inside me. I cried. After all my sacrifices I'd ended up alone on the roof. I went to the edge, suddenly tempted to finish it all. But I went back down the stairs to find Imane, who saved me from insanity. She put her arms around me, she started to talk to me the way she did before, once more forming the bubble around us in which we'd aways felt good. I'd found her again. She had a good head on her shoulders and once again had used it to pass on some of her strength to me. Her warmth consoled me, it reconciled me to her.

But the fracture was still there. Despite my immense relief, I continued to feel it. Like a pain in my heart, like a loss impossible to ignore. I couldn't resume my life as if nothing had happened. So I capitulated. I put on the great *djellaba* that covers your body, I tied a veil around my face and I went to the mosque—I even kept on going there every day. I thought I'd found the solution: to become like everyone else.

I suggested to the mosque authorities that I should take on the children's education, and they accepted on condition that I limited myself to teaching them religion. The girls were eleven or twelve, they called me Aunt Asmaa. My course consisted of an interpretation of the verses of the Koran. For example, I told them the story of Joseph, *sayedna* Youssef, beautiful as the moon, whom his master's wife accused of having assaulted her, giving as proof the handsome young man's torn shirt. I didn't say that his master's wife had wanted to sleep with Joseph and he'd run off leaving her holding his shirt but simply, "She liked him," so that the girls understood without being shocked. I also talked to them about Abraha the Ethiopian, who came with his elephants to destroy the Kaaba, also mentioning that the holy stone was in fact prior to Islam. That is perhaps my function in life: to tell stories, whether they are religious or not. I didn't stop there, I suggested the girls should take part in a cultural quiz: "Who is the writer who wrote such and such a book? Who is the most famous Arabic poet?" They loved it! During the breaks a little boy came to sell chewing gum by the door and the girls bought some.

The women officials at the mosque didn't like anything I did: my interpretations of the Koran annoyed them, my cultural quiz wasn't very *halal*[2] and giving the girls permission to go out to buy candy from a street kid didn't please them either. I had to limit myself to the Koran and to religious explanations, period. In my innocence I was surprised at their reaction: to my eyes nothing in my behavior or in my explanations contradicted our religion. I had put on a veil and returned to the mosque but these women were pushing me away. Basically they had nothing to do with Islam. When I went to pray, they told me, "You're not doing it the proper way, the position of your hand isn't right, your right hand has to be on top of your left, your elbows must not touch the ground," etc., etc. The essential thing for me was how my heart was to come to pray, but they had no idea of that. It was only the rituals, the practices that were important for them, not feelings. I couldn't even see that they were rejecting me. It was no use me putting on long skirts, all-covering smocks, a complete hijab, they continued to look askance at me.

One day when we were going out on an excursion I went to buy some biscuits before joining them. I telephoned to tell them I'd be a little late and they said, "The bus will wait for

2 *halal*: lawful, according to Islam; *haram*: unlawful, forbidden

you." When I arrived there was no one there. It was only at that point that I realized they didn't want me to be on the trip. The girls on the bus were upset by that but not the officials, far from it. The realization was a blow but at last I'd gotten the message. I didn't go back to the mosque, I came back to my senses. Actually I'd just discovered Mustafa Mahmoud, a Marxist Egyptian author, who had turned to Islam, a very moderate Islam. I started to read him and to think I'd been stupid. I took off my religious clothes and dressed as I had before.

My father had been shaving when I'd told him, "Father, I'm going to dress like a believer."

He almost cut himself and replied, "No!"

I said it wasn't his business, etc., and he remained silent.

Once again he was in the bathroom. "Father, I'm going to dress as I used to."

"No!"

"Listen. I know an American poet who said, 'I'm not ashamed of a truth I've come to, even if it contradicts the previous one.'"

He fell silent again. I continued to read Mustafa Mahmoud, I returned to Ghada al-Samman, and I reinforced my personality. This period was certainly a turning point for me. My uncles lost no time in going on the attack. "Why have you taken off your believer's clothes, what path are you embarking on?"

"When a religious boy changes, no one notices because his clothes remain the same, while with us girls everyone realizes because it can be seen from our clothes."

It wasn't a great argument and I don't imagine it convinced them, but I didn't care: at last I had become myself again.

12

The Islamic University

DESPITE MY SATISFACTORY grades in the year-end exams—76/100—German universities didn't want me, on the pretext that Palestinian girls would only come to Germany in order to get married and not to study. Faced with such a sexist rejection there was nothing for it but to go to the Islamic university in Gaza, to the Journalism and Information Department. My father wasn't unhappy with my choice; he himself taught at the university that was known to be close to Hamas. I was soon getting good results, even though I was constantly arguing with the staff. I was summoned to the disciplinary committee. My 'judge' was the head of Student Affairs, Atallah Abu Sbeih, who was later to become minister of culture in the Hamas government before being appointed minister of prisoners.

"They tell me that you've been taking books by Ghada al-Samman and Ghassan Kanafani to class and have been reading from them publicly to other women students..."

"That is true."

"And that you discuss them with the others..."

"Yes, certainly. Where's the problem?"

"You know very well where it is."

"Ghassan is in love with Ghada, who doesn't respond to him. Furious, he writes to her, 'May your religion be cursed.' Is that what's bothering you?"

"Yes, it's that. I see that you are aware of the problem."

"Of course I'm aware of it. But it's literature!"

I was very stubborn. He spent two hours arguing with me without getting anywhere. Then he changed the subject: "When you wear an *abaya* (a long cloak), your arms can be seen... you ought to have a long-sleeved blouse underneath."

I was dumbstruck. That was the Islamic University. At a minimum you had to have a scarf over your head, long sleeves, trousers under your dress, no make-up, and of course the girls were separated from the boys. It was the biggest university in the territory and had thousands of women students, all consenting apart from me. My 'judge' went to see my father, saying, "I've never come across a mind like that of your daughter, she reads and argues endlessly. Could I come to your house to talk to her?"

My father said, "Yes, come." We sat in the parlor and he started, "When you see a young man and a young woman together, do you think they're talking about the peace process?"

"Why not?"

I gave as good as I got. Basically what he was saying could be summed up as a long list of what one ought or ought not do.

"It's up to me to say what I think and what I feel, not to anyone else. It's up to me to decide what's good and what's bad, not Student Affairs. God Himself counts on human beings' free will. It's not the place of the University to say how I must dress—otherwise you should establish a uniform for all, just as at kindergarten."

He left without getting anywhere. I clashed with the professor of Arabic literature, who claimed I was afraid of arguing with him. Then it was the turn of the professor of political science who handed out to us a book on the Islamic parties in Muslim society. I refused to take it, preferring to pursue my own research in the library. I came across a book by Yusuf al Qaradawi, a famous sheikh and member of the Muslim Brotherhood, who claimed that 'Muslim society' didn't exist, there was solely a 'society containing Muslims' with the result that no one could consider Islam as their monopoly. Convinced by his argumentation, I finished my research and handed in my essay. The professor went mad. He argued with me in front of the class as if I was alone with him. He maintained that the Muslim State should accept no other party than the Islamic Party because power naturally resides in the hands of the emir. And if another party existed, it should also be Islamic. He was in total disagreement with me, even though he gave me a good mark, 92/100. I was very encouraged by the fact that he respected my opinion despite his personal opposition. Despite that, I found the atmosphere in that university unbearable. After putting up with it for two years I couldn't stand it any longer and decided to change.

My father wouldn't hear of it. "If you go to another university I won't pay your fees anymore."

"Don't pay for anything anymore. As the writer Gamal al Ghitani says, 'The migraine of liberty is better than the cancer of oppression.'"

He continued to put pressure on me but I didn't give way. In 2002 I went to the secular Al Azhar University, in the department that my Uncle Ahmed, the owner of the library, had chosen before me: Arabic Language and Literature. It took me an hour and a half every day to get from Rafah to my college in the city of Gaza. I also had to find paid work, my father having carried out his threat.

At my new university the academic level was low but the professors were great. I would discuss the history and problems of the language with them, I really loved that. The university itself had both a conservative and a liberal tradition which were constantly at loggerheads. They were absolutely contrary to each other but they created a space for discussion. It was a change for me from the monolithic thought prevailing at the Islamic University. I led groups on literary education in which we discussed forms and techniques of writing with the other female students—it was fascinating.

In order to survive, I worked as a sales assistant in a clothes shop. I and some other girls rented a shared apartment, which spared me the exhausting return journeys. The experience of cohabitation was enjoyable and taught us independence. And what was more, we lived by the sea. I fairly soon gave up my job as saleswoman: the newspaper *Ramadan Daily* gave me my first experience of journalism. I also got an internship with a sports paper and wrote articles for it that were always signed with a man's name. When I asked why, the editor replied, "Because it's shameful to give a woman a byline in a sports paper aimed exclusively at men." I resigned.

Unfortunately there were only three women students who had registered for Arabic Language and Literature. Judging the number insufficient, the University took the decision to suspend the course. I didn't know what to do. I started working for *Al Quds* newspaper, but the manager, who liked what I wrote very much, didn't even pay my travel costs. I wore the same trousers for three years; my father still wasn't giving me a cent. I was angry at him—without realizing that his obstinacy was good for me: it taught me to fend for myself. I wrote short stories for various journals that paid me 100 shekels each—the equivalent of $25. I continued with this balancing act until the day in 1991 when I came across a fairly correct magazine from the Emirates: *Woman of Today*. I sent a letter of application and they replied that they could take me on for the "Culture and

Society" section. I was nineteen; one year later I had the means to open an office. It was the first time a journalist in Gaza had anything like that.

The office went well and I was soon earning enough money to pay the rent. I was sharing with two associates: one who worked for *The Gulf* newspaper, the other for *Al Quds*; both were members of Hamas. The *Gulf* writer and I were discussing religion all the time and that was great, but the other one didn't like either my independence or my visitors, and he had forbidden his employees to talk to me. I was isolated but I couldn't care less about that. Despite everything, I would have loved my family to leave the house in Rafah and come and live in Gaza. I did talk about that to my father but he resisted the suggestion. My sister Aïsha was grown up and she was even more obstinate than me. Not only did she refuse to cover her head but she had adopted a dog that followed her everywhere—no one likes dogs around there. And it wasn't just her. My other sisters were also growing up in a conservative neighborhood where people were starting to look askance at them. Suddenly my father had had enough of this society where you're supposed to marry off your daughters at fourteen—and him with six of them! Overnight he decided to move the whole family to Gaza.

We rented an ordinary house in the Zeitoun district of Gaza, then another in the Tel al Hawa district, where we started all living together again. Things had changed. In the absence of my uncles, my father felt he was invested with some power or other over me. He interfered in my affairs, in my work, my comings and goings. For my part I reproached him for his lack of trust in me. He was no longer the father I knew. One day we argued and he started to cry. As for me, I will keep arguing right to the end without ever crying—and he was the one who taught me that: "Your tears," he told me, "will never make me change my mind." And I couldn't bear to see him in tears out in the street. The arguments, the cries, the difficulties, all the pressures were having an effect on me—I definitely had to find a way of freeing myself.

It was at that moment that my magazine, *Woman of Today*, invited me to a meeting in Cairo that several of their journalists would be attending. It was the first time in my life that I went to Cairo by myself. There I met the editor, Kamal, a truly charming Egyptian, the very image of the man I could have in mind: a poet, left-wing, not giving a damn about anything, never judging... I fell in love with him at once. When I got back to Gaza, he telephoned my father to ask for my hand in marriage. But neither my father nor my family wanted to have anything to do with him. He was divorced and seventeen years older than me. That didn't bother me at all, I was suffocating in my life, my father was keeping a close eye on me and trying the restrict my freedom. Kamal gave me the possibility of escaping, I was ready to follow him to the Emirates, where he lived. Some of my uncles who lived in the Gulf enquired about him—they were told he was a good man. I loved him, or perhaps I just loved the kind of man who corresponded to my fantasy. I also wanted to forget Saleh, my English teacher, to expel him from my memories for good.

We got engaged in Gaza. I refused to accept a *mahr* (the equivalent of a dowry given to the fiancée) because I didn't believe that a woman had a price. Even the sheikh who was to marry us was surprised at my refusal. I pointed out that the Prophet had said, "The higher their virtue, the lower their mahr will be," which I translated as: the best woman will not take a *mahr* at all. But the sheikh didn't agree, no more than my father or my uncles. The *mahr* was the equivalent of $3500, to which a further $3500 had to be added for the *mou'akhar* (a sum kept in reserve) and $3500 for the furniture, for a total of $10,500. I said again that I didn't want it and my father accepted my argument. We organized a little party without music—I don't really believe in that kind of ceremony—and that was all. We got married before leaving for the Emirates via Egypt. That was in 2003.

13

With My Back to the Screen

I CAME BACK FROM this second stay in the Emirates with a child and a book, the only two good things that happened to me there. Otherwise it was a catastrophe. Even on our honeymoon in Cairo I woke up no longer knowing who I was. My head was throbbing with depression. Kamal was an irresponsible person. He didn't hit me, didn't insult me, behaved like a gentleman; on the other hand, however, he had absolutely no concern for things that made me suffer. We had only just gotten there when we learnt that *Woman of Today* didn't allow a husband and wife to work in the same editorial office. So I resigned and stayed at home while he spent his time out of the house. Fortunately he had a large library in which I discovered Marcuse, the Turkish writer Pamuk, Süskind's *Perfume*, a marvelous biography of T. S. Eliot translated by an Iraqi... There were also a lot of films, the whole of Iranian cinema. But Kamal sometimes came home late at night...

"Papa, Mama, that man is so harsh it stuns me, that's not the man I married, that's a stranger! I've destroyed my life, given up my work, my office, I've fled one reality for another that's ten times worse, love is nothing but a lie. I'm an idiot, a child, I'm only twenty-one!" I was buying phone cards by the packet, my parents listened to me and cried, tried to talk to me gently. No one could calm me down.

I very quickly became pregnant. I felt I was caught in a trap but I found it impossible to accept the situation and resign myself to it. When I was four months pregnant I took the plane to Gaza. Kamal started phoning my father every day to get me to go back. I did love him and I went back, but it was hopeless. His good resolutions only lasted a few days. My mother came to stay with me for the birth, she could see my sad situation with her own eyes. One evening she tried to drag me out to the cinema to take my mind off things. To my great surprise Kamal decided to go with us. The film was a comedy with the well-known Egyptian actor Adel Imam. Half way through I could feel my water breaking. My mother and Kamal wouldn't believe me, they wanted to see the rest of the film and advised me to go to the toilet. I don't know what happened to me but I climbed up onto the stage and stood with my back to the screen, facing the audience. I was afraid, I didn't know what to do. Suddenly I saw Kamal and Mama rushing up, one took my right hand, the other my left and they dragged me out. In the light you could see that my white dress was soaked with the water of the baby. I reached the maternity ward at nine in the evening. Fifteen minutes later Nasser was beside me, delivered by Cesarian section— otherwise his life would have been in danger. The African midwife handed him to me and said in English, "Your baby."

The nurses started joking. "Since he was born in the cinema your son might become a great director or a famous actor."

"Unless he ends up sweeping out the cinema," I replied, and everyone laughed.

His birth didn't really sort things out between Kamal and me. I took up my pen and started to write my first collection of short stories. The first one is called "Your Baby." It's about that moment, Nasser's arrival and the inevitable separation from his father. Despite everything, I continued to make an effort, but not him. Nasser was three months old, I gathered my things together, took my baby in my arms and slammed the door. I stayed in the Emirates but took refuge with my uncles. I awoke every morning to find I'd left some hairs on the pillow. I said I was going to consult a doctor when in fact it was an Iraqi psychiatrist I went to see. He advised me to return to my normal life, that is to writing, to get as far away as possible from the world of the child, from feeding, from Pampers and company. According to him, if I were to devote myself to my son it would be a symbolic admission that to my mind my life was over. I obeyed without arguing.

Kamal had kept my passport and Nasser's. After six months and repeated requests, I realized that he would never release me. I went to the house at a time when I knew he wouldn't be in. Biti was there, a young African woman who worked for us and whom I liked very much. We used to go out together to a café called *La Brioche*. She also worked for her Emirati 'guarantor' who took 1000 dirhams a month from her (about $330) as the price of his 'guarantee'. She paid so that he wouldn't get her thrown out of the country—a man who spent all his time in the mosque! And she, as a Christian, had to wear the *'abaya* whenever she went to see that pious man, otherwise he would insult her. Such is the despicable regime in the Gulf states. So Biti opened the door for me and her eyes were shining. I took the passports and fled.

Before taking the plane I phoned Kamal to tell him I was leaving. He started crying. I let him go on for a while then asked him whether we could see each other for a moment, have a coffee together. He came, we met, and there I read him "Segregation on a Blackboard," which was going to be the title story of the collection. It's the story of a woman who every day writes down what happens to her and ends up leaving her poet husband who is driving her mad. He liked it. We started to talk as two writers, forgetting we were husband and wife and that I was about to leave him. When the time arrived, I stood up, took Nasser in my arms and we parted. On the plane I told myself that I, for my part, had perhaps been a burden to Kamal. I had been living with the depression that had taken hold of me during our honeymoon and had not let go of me for the following eighteen months. I had been unhappy and on my guard all the time. I had given him the chance to change our relationship but he hadn't taken it. He would say to me, "I'd go around the world barefoot for you, Asmaa," and it was true that he loved me, I was well aware of that. But he couldn't change. In his poetry you could feel how he was attracted to madness and the void. That was in May 2005. Two months later he sent me the papers allowing me to get a divorce with no problem. A true gentleman, as I said.

14

The Taste of Mangoes

IN GAZA MY FATHER said to me, "I dreamed that I was the one who was bringing up your son." And that was in fact what he was doing. Our relationship, which was strained when I got married, had been restored thanks to Nasser. I took the medicines the Iraqi psychiatrist had prescribed to reduce my heartbeat and vitamins for my hair. After a while my father asked me, "Why are you taking medicine? You're stronger than that." I gave them up and cut my hair.

I met two very dear friends who welcomed me back: Saleh, who was in charge of a human rights organization, and Suhail, who was a lawyer. Nowadays we're constantly arguing because they close their eyes to the machinations of Hamas a little too often—as does the nation as a whole moreover. But I will never forget how they opened doors for me when I came back from the Emirates, divorced and desperate. They gave me back my self-confidence at a time when my name had been forgotten. Under the auspices of his organization, Saleh offered to set up a review for the defense of human rights: *Al Damir* ('Conscience'); ten years later it's still appearing, true to its original aims. Suhail, whom I'd gotten to know at Abul Hôli, the Israeli checkpoint between Gaza and the south, introduced me to his many friends. I started working again, meeting people, writing. That same year, 2005, *Al Ayyam* ran a competition to recruit a journalist. That daily newspaper was a dream for me: I admired it when I was sixteen and had published my first poem in it. In the end I won the competition! My first article was about a film by the Egyptian director Yousry Nasrallah, *The Gate of the Sun.* The editor who published it sent me a message from Ramallah: "We don't want a cinema critic but a journalist." So I started going out and about.

A bomb had been thrown at a wedding and killed a fourteen-year-old kid—the only boy among nine girls. I met the victim's parents and was told that the family that had organized the ceremony had made the mistake of celebrating the wedding by playing music, which the Islamists regarded as a sin. Fatah and the Palestinian Authority were still in power in Gaza but Hamas, in opposition at the time, was having a growing influence on attitudes. That is what I wrote about in the opening section of the article on the affair. During my inquiries I discovered that those who had thrown the bomb were very young and regular attenders at a mosque run by Hamas. The sheikh whose teachings they followed was convinced that the rest of society was made up of unbelievers. Wearing a very long dress and a hijab, I asked to speak to the imam and was taken to him. I felt I had to be very direct.

"Did you teach the young boys who threw the bomb?"

"They used to come to the mosque, that is true, and we did teach them..."

At that moment the *khatib* (the one who gives the sermons) intervened brusquely. He demanded to see my press card, to know who I was, what I was doing there, and I quickly realized that he was trying to make me out to be a 'spy.' In a flash, a hostile and threatening crowd had gathered around me. I was very much afraid but I remained calm. I repeated that I was a journalist, flourished my press card and managed to get away. That scene was, of course, the subject of the second section of my article. The next day, a Friday, someone telephoned me from the mosque to warn me that the *khatib* was talking about me while he was preaching. He let me hear the sermon as it was being given: "A journalist, a corrupt, indecent woman, came to tell us what's what..." I immediately wrote the third section of my article, which was published the next day, citing the sermon word for word. The *khatib* went mad. He had no idea I could have been informed so quickly and so precisely. He was afraid. All this could turn into a conflict between his family and mine: my status as a woman abused in public meant I could assert my rights, in particular to ask my family to protect me against him. He therefore went to the newspaper offices to justify himself, claiming I went to the mosque in order to provoke him. I wasn't there. The managing director saw him, no one from the editorial staff. When I was informed of this, I let the *khatib* know that I had no intention of talking to my family about this because I alone was responsible for my actions.

The people from Hamas, accompanied by the mayor of the family, knocked on the door of the parents of the boy who had been killed. They gave them a little money to compensate them and that was the end of the matter. It had been turned into a family matter and the Party had resolved the conflict. This affair is typical of the inhabitants of Gaza. In the end it is often the mayor of the family who is responsible for resolving conflicts. When a woman who has been beaten by her husband reports to the police, they contact the mayor, who takes the woman home. There's no law, as there is in the West, nothing like that. The mayor, elected by the families or designated by elected local assemblies, is responsible for everyone as if he were the father of them all. He tells you what you must do and you do it. But why do we need mayors instead of judges? Why this tribal system?

My next subject was much more political: Israel had announced a unilateral retreat from the Gaza Strip. I finally met the journalists—Palestinians and foreigners—who were working in the territory, a little band of editors, photographers, cameramen, drivers and interpreters, who had often been working alongside each other for years. In that milieu no one knew me yet. It was during the summer of 2005. I wanted to get as far out as possible, right to the edge of the settlements without worrying about possible danger. We all went there. I saw settlers who had climbed up on the roofs with their children to resist being evacuated by the Israeli army. And how they cried—they'd lined up gas canisters and were threatening to blow themselves up. Leaving their land was out of the question for them. The situation seemed dangerous. "But why are they so angry?" I asked myself. "What does this land mean to them?"

They seemed to have reached the peak of suffering, and I had an incredulous smile on my face. I wasn't making fun of them; no, no one was insulting them. I was simply astonished at the strangeness of the situation. It was a historic moment and we were experiencing it from inside history, but there was a kind of scent of *it can't be true*. I couldn't believe that the settlers were really going to withdraw and allow us to take back our land.

However, they did do so and almost without resistance. On that day I was driving with other journalists. We zigzagged our way through the empty settlements. The occupiers had gone without leaving anything behind them, everything was flattened, everything had been destroyed, the houses, the public buildings, the schools... All that was left were the mango trees they'd planted, and we devoured the fruit—excellent! The population of Gaza had prepared for the event. As soon as possible, hundreds of people descended on the evacuated territory to pick up anything that was worth picking up: electric wires for the copper, landline telephones left on the ground, door frames, plumbing, pieces of broken toilets... I wrote an article on this poor raid that followed the evacuation of the settlements but the editor refused to publish it. He wanted a nice picture, a dignified liberation. I pointed out that the reality was precisely as I had described it—he wouldn't listen. It was my first dispute with the paper.

Very soon Hamas was shouting from the rooftops, "We've liberated Gaza!" unconcerned about the fact that according to international law Gaza still had the status of occupied territory. What is more, it was Yasser Arafat's Fatah that was in power at the time. I said to myself, "Both Fatah and Hamas are trying to pull the wool over our eyes, neither of them have liberated anything at all." We thought Arafat had scored a victory, but Jerusalem had not been liberated and the famous 'safe passage' to the West Bank foreseen in the Oslo Accords had not been opened. In Gaza, the farmers who had been able to produce title deeds did recover their plots, which have since become agricultural land again. On the other hand, in many other parts, especially private estates designated as "liberated lands," Hamas was to install military training camps once it took over power in 2007. The Islamic Jihad and others were to do the same. Veritable new towns were to see the light of day: Asda' el I'lamiye, Nur el Tarfihiye, very beautiful towns, surrounded by greenery, but empty. Later a branch of the University of Al Aqsa would be built there in which the students spent their days but returned home to sleep in their parents' houses. Unveiled women were to be implicitly forbidden from entering those towns even though there is no Palestinian law formally obliging any woman to cover her head.

All the same, we once more had access to the finest

beach, in place of the one they'd left to us. The settlers had naturally appropriated the best places, the greenest regions, planted with trees, the most fertile land, the purest water. Once in power Hamas was able to get its hands on the main part of all that. Another innovation: there was no longer the Israeli checkpoint between north and south where you could sometimes get stuck for hours on end—a real liberation! Lovers lost their best alibi: in Gaza it's impossible for a young woman to meet a young man in a café. When a father accused his daughter of talking to some man, she would say, "We were waiting at the checkpoint together." I didn't have a lover, I made do with watching the couples from afar. The profit for me was limited. I hadn't taken anything from the settlements nor gained anything from the withdrawal—but I had eaten the mangoes!

15

Special Group

NOW THE POLLING STATIONS are closed, it's the evening. We're in the offices of a human rights organization in order to follow, hour by hour, the count of the vote that has just taken place both on the West Bank and in Gaza. It's 2006. I'd spent my time walking around the streets asking questions for *Al Ayyam*. The women told me, "We don't want anything more to do with Fatah. We're fed up with them." I asked, "And the Popular Front?" to which they replied, "Who? Those unbelievers? No way." Every time I came across a member of Hamas, I would shout out, "You're not going to win!" I walked around the town saying to my friends, "God forbid that Hamas should win. If they do I'll take off my veil!"—Since my marriage to Kamal I had returned to the 'demi-hijab', letting my hair show. I was joking, my veil had nothing to do with Hamas, I was simply being provocative.

But I was still worried. Everywhere I could see how perfectly the Islamist party was mobilizing its vote. Its militants were present everywhere, going to collect people from their homes or meeting them at the tables and chairs they had put out around the polling station. Their campaign had been aimed above all at the very poor, they had gone to help them, arranged for their education and partly opened the doors of the Islamic University for them. They had played it as the Iranians had done before them and seemed to have won the voters' hearts in a much more intelligent way than the Egyptian Muslim Brotherhood. I saw the women, who wanted nothing more to do with Fatah, filling the mosques during the campaign. If there was a class on religion, they would all rush over to attend. But if a meeting was organized by the very secular Committee for Women's Rights, no one went. Why had Hamas been so convincing? Because people, including myself, were weary of the corruption of the present government. When I was at university there were the children of Fatah dignitaries all around me, sons of generals, sons of high officials, sons of officers who all lived in sumptuous villas and received—at fifteen or sixteen—salaries between $1000 to $2000 dollars a month for doing nothing! The secular university of Al Azhar belonged to Fatah—that is, to themselves. Coming from the miserable Islamic university I felt ashamed to go to classes with those girls with their smart hair-dos, the latest model of cell phone in their hand, their car in the parking lot by the gate. In those days, I used to remind myself that their fathers were imprisoning left-wing and Islamic militants by the dozen. They forced them to sing songs contrary to their convictions, humiliated them, tortured them, sometimes even killed them.

To be fair, Arafat himself was not corrupt, but he had corrupted all those around him. It was said that one of them had set up the company that had sold Israel the millions of tons of cement they needed to construct the wall separating Israel and the West Bank. It was also said that on every liter of fuel sold at any gas station in the Palestinian territories a 'commission' was paid directly into the personal bank account of another one, who is a billionaire today. But where did this money come from? Before the Oslo Accords, when all of you from Fatah were dispersed in Tunisia, in Libya or elsewhere, when Arafat was surrounded, you couldn't even manage to pay our salaries! The big businessmen, the Palestinians who had companies, took pity on you and gave you a few cents so that you could survive. Then suddenly, after Oslo, there was no end of money! The stupid European Union and the even more stupid United States paid billions to support your Palestinian 'Authority'. The people got nothing from this, just a few crumbs, all the rest ended up in your pockets!

The first results arrive at the Human Rights office: Hamas is making great gains, but Fatah is putting up more resistance than one would have thought. Their militants go out into the streets and start firing their Kalashnikovs in the air to persuade themselves that they're going to win. But the next results douse their hopes: Hamas is in the lead everywhere. And we, the left-wingers, secular voters, liberals, moderate Muslims are wringing our hands in despair— "They're going to win!" We can't even cast doubt on the integrity of the poll: the foreign observers have found nothing wrong, ex-President Carter is there, everything seems to be in order. By one in the morning we realize there is no hope. I go home and fall asleep watching the television. I'm woken by telephone calls from my friends: "They've won, it's all over!" and I say, "Oh God! A curse on you all, this time they're going to destroy us." I dash out into the street like a madwoman. Unveiled! But this isn't just a joke. The people who see me pass bareheaded are astonished but I tell them, "Hamas is winning—do you think I'm going to stay veiled? I prefer to take off my veil before they force me to keep it on."

I knew Hamas from having grown up with it, from having lived in close quarters with that 'morality' made up of conservatism and rules of behavior that are supposedly Islamic—but in reality are as alien to the religion as they are to any real spirituality. If the corruption of Fatah had been repelling, the rigidity of Hamas wasn't much better. People were aware of this, if somewhat confused: they didn't put out the flags because of the victory of the Islamist movement, far from it, they were simply happy that Fatah had lost—but they were just as concerned, or almost, at the prospect of domination by Hamas. A more or less unanimous demand very quickly made itself heard: "We want a Fatah-Hamas government of national unity." The leaders of the two groups saw the way the wind was blowing: a coalition government was quickly formed and people could breathe again. But it was clear that the country was sitting on a powder-keg.

Then the masks started to come off. Officials who were thought to be loyal to Fatah, among them one of my cousins, neighbors, people I would never have suspected, suddenly let their beards grow. Hamas supporters became more visible, showing that there were a lot more of them than one could imagine. And what was worse, it became clear that the administrators of the Authority had voted for Hamas in a much higher proportion than the population in general. The Fatah leadership could not remain indifferent and immediately instigated more or less open warfare with the intention of suppressing Hamas. That was not easy since the military wing of the Islamist movement, the al Qassam Brigades, was well established. Fatah therefore set up a "Special Group," several members of which are in exile today. I wonder why certain European governments have granted them citizenship. Their mission in Gaza was simply to kill, to torture and to exert all kinds of bloody pressure on Hamas supporters. One of the members of this "Special Group" lived quite close to us; Hamas was entrenched on the other side, in the university district. Our block was thus in the middle of the battle that was going on over our heads and outside our houses with pistol shots, bursts of Kalashnikov fire and exchanges of shells. I was working in my room one day when a bomb landed right on our balcony—without exploding, otherwise we'd all have been dead.

One morning in the offices of *Al Ayyam* a message from the Korean National Institute for Translation appeared on the screen of my computer: I had been granted a six-month writer's residency in South Korea—the Palestinian writer Adania Shibli had supported my application. My initial reaction was to say that six months was perhaps too long but was very quickly replaced by, "After all why shouldn't I go? What is there to keep me here?" Thus, one April morning in 2007 I turned up with my suitcase at the border in Rafah to try and cross into Egypt in order to travel to far-off Korea. Following the agreement that had previously been negotiated, the crossing was controlled by Europeans and an immense crowd of Palestinians was pushing to try and get across the damn border. I shouted, "I'm by myself, let me out!" I have no idea by what miracle the barrier was raised but I found myself on the other side, in a bus bound for Cairo. The barrier closed immediately behind me for eight long months. I had gotten out at the very last moment.

The next day I was on a plane that took sixteen hours to get to its destination, after a short stopover in Hong Kong. The doors opened, I looked around, I was in Korea. The people all looked the same—a stupid first impression, of course. I remember having said to myself, "What the hell am I doing here? What is this strange country I've come to?"

16

Is This the Country We Want?

THIS ISN'T A COUNTRY, it's a garden. Seventy per cent of the mountains in Korea are covered in trees. The room I have in the student residence in Hankuk University is quiet, I can see trees when I look out. I've been in Korea for two months now. Strife has broken out in Gaza, Hamas supporters have taken all the Palestinian Authority's positions throughout the territory by storm. They threw a man off the top of an apartment block fifteen stories high and committed some terrible crimes; it is said that they have assassinated over two hundred members of Fatah.

I've learnt Korean in a short time and immersed myself in the literature and cinema of the country. The language, the food, the people—everything is fascinating here. I'm 8000 kilometers away from Gaza and two hours by road from Seoul: out in the middle of nowhere! Fatah had its share of responsibility: encouraged by the Americans, they went for a confrontation. Now they'd been attacked, they had no option but to respond. The battle was raging with automatic rifles and rocket-launchers, no one was in control of anything anymore. In the residence I'm the only person from the Middle East among authors from all over the world. I talk to everyone in English, a dictionary in my hand. I establish relations with Ketso, a South African writer slightly older than me. I ask her if it's true that AIDS is present all over South Africa and she replies, "Of course, it's flying through the air" and is angry with me. I go and apologize. She'd made me feel I had traces of racism inside me without realizing it.

In a panic, I call my parents. My father tells me that Hamas militants twice went up on our roof looking for armed men, they burst into the house of Mahmoud Abbas, the head of the Palestinian Authority, and had themselves photographed sitting triumphantly at his desk.

I'm stunned: until then Hamas had been a political grouping that demanded respect for a so-called Islamic morality and had so far never shed any Palestinian blood. Far away in Korea I feel that it is a historical mistake to inaugurate a 'reign' with a bloodbath of one's own people because Fatah is the people as well. Abbas launched an appeal for an end to the confrontation. In reality the battle was already lost for him because Hamas controlled the whole of the Gaza Strip. The vague justification they put forward by talking about a 'decisive movement' rather than a 'coup d'état' doesn't hold water. They reminded people of their victory in the municipal elections of 2005 that had been annulled by the Palestinian Authority; they cited the example of Algeria where, at the beginning of the nineties, the Islamic Salvation Front had been deprived of its electoral success in the same way. Therefore, they claimed, they had taken 'preventive action' for fear of having their victory in the 2006 parliamentary elections stolen in the same way. That is why they went on a spree of killing, expelling, humiliating, and parading the hundreds of Fatah members they'd made prisoners—some are still in prison to this day. Those who emigrated, those who lost their houses, those who bowed down to Hamas to be allowed to leave the territory must also be counted among their victims...

I had found work as a waitress in a Palestinian restaurant in Seoul. I went there every weekend. The owners—two brothers—paid me 4000 wons per hour (about 4 dollars), less than the Korean minimum wage. One of them claimed to be religious and prayed five times a day. They said I drove their customers away because I discussed politics with them and put on CDs by the Lebanese singer Fairuz rather than the music of the Gulf that their rich Saudi customers liked. On the telephone my father told me that Uncle Saïd, the head of what was called the "Executive"—Hamas' security organization in Rafah—had deposited with our family material taken from the institutions dependent on Fatah. He also locked up a number of militants there as well, and they were clearly maltreated—neighbors complained to my parents about the cries they heard.

I learn that the coup d'état has led to the shutting down of all the Gaza borders, with Israel as well as with Egypt. So the crimes are taking place behind closed doors. The horrors that are happening in the house where I spent my adolescence—my uncles built it with their own hands—go around and around in my head. I'm devastated. After several days without being able to sleep, I write, "Is this the country we want, Uncle?" The letter is addressed to my Uncle Saïd, head of the Executive in Rafah. In it I recall the memories of my childhood, the family house we all shared, the episode of the dolls destroyed to please him, the deep love binding me to him despite our almost complete differences of opinion. "But what Hamas and the Executive you're in charge of are doing in Rafah today, Uncle, are things even the enemy didn't do! In three days you've killed more militants than Israel did in several months. [...] Have you thought of the message you're sending us? Are you offering us an Islamic State built on the corpses and souls of those who belong to us? [...] I'm trying to find excuses because I love you, but I can't. [...] You have ordered your men to exact vengeance and take control of everything—as if we were infidels. [...] Do you know what hurts me the most, Uncle dear? It's what you've done to our family house in Rafah. [...] That house was open to all [...] and Gaza was the home to Fatah, as well as to Hamas or the Popular Front, the home of the believer as well as the non-believer, of the veiled woman as well as one who goes bareheaded. [...] Despite everything, I still think that you aren't that hard man with no pity for his victims, nor the bloodthirsty man you're trying to become. You are my beloved uncle, and I would have liked to have been able to say goodbye to you before setting off for the distant country where I am at the moment. But I was afraid of seeing the change that has happened within you, I was afraid that my simple presence beside you would have made me complicit in the criminal Executive of which you are in charge."

The letter is there before me, hand-written, but how can I send it? I don't have a laptop. It's the weekend, I walk through the streets of Seoul asking people if they know where I can find a computer with an Arabic keyboard. I'm told about an Internet café, the *Casablanca*. I walk for a long time. The boss is a Moroccan who admires Israel. He starts teasing me as soon as he learns that I'm Palestinian. I tell him, "I haven't come to talk politics, I'm just looking for a computer." He says, "You see that guy sitting over there, the one with glasses wearing a skullcap? Go and ask him, he'll know."

I introduce myself and explain my problem. He's called Sohaib. He's Moroccan as well and we have to talk in literary Arabic. I sit down beside him. Not only does he help me, he corrects my letter as well. He knows the Koran by heart and has a language that is a thousand times better than mine, an ancient, classical language—but which he handles in a very modern manner. We finish writing it, reread it, I thank him and send off the letter to my father at once so that he can print it out and pass it on to my Uncle Saïd. I also send a copy to a friend. My father calls me next morning:

"Your uncle's read your letter and he burst out laughing. He told me you spent too much time watching *Falastine*, the Fatah channel."

"But I'm in Korea, how could I receive that channel? *Al Jazeera*'s the only one I watch. And anyway, my letter has nothing to do with Fatah."

Twenty-four hours later I discover that my piece is on the Internet and that it's already been read twenty thousand times. My phone in the residence never stops ringing; I get back to my parents and they tell me that they too have been inundated with calls: "Your daughter has expressed our anger; she's allowed us to recover our pride."—"She's said what we all feel deep down inside"—"She's made us feel better"—"We were just hoping someone would have the courage to say things like that"—because until then everyone had kept their mouths shut. Put to fire and the sword by Hamas, Gaza submitted and I threw the bomb from the antipodes. There were soon thousands of comments on the Net.

Relatives, neighbors, acquaintances are all asking me the same question, "Who posted your letter on the Internet?" I'd told my father that it wasn't me. As the days passed the question became more and more insistent: "Come on, tell us. We want to know!" It's impossible for me to reply without endangering the friend to whom I sent a copy. By now, my uncle's mood had changed. Very annoyed, he and his brothers decided to boycott my parents. If they met them, they turned their backs and didn't speak to them. And suddenly my father had an SMS on his phone: "Tell your daughter she'd better not come back from South Korea because we're going to kill her." It's the first time in my life I've received a message like that. A little later my Uncle Saïd posted a comment on the Net that began thus, "Aouad al-Ghoul (my father), his sons and his daughters, whose ideas are alien to Islam..." In other words, he was washing his hands in advance of anything that might happen to us. The pressure was such that I eventually called the editor of the site that had posted my letter. He was a Palestinian who had fled Hamas to settle in London:

"Remove my letter, for God's sake, my parents are being threatened..."

"Why do you think I should remove it? Tens of thousands of people have visited my site thanks to your letter. I will not remove it."

"At least suppress the comments that insult me."

He agrees to do that. Other reactions showed a certain ambivalence. I heard, for example, that the imam of the Rafah mosque, Nazi el-Loka, a supporter of Hamas, had quoted and commented on my letter in his Friday sermon. He had begun by saying some more favorable things about it and finished with, "But talking about love is reserved for women."

I would very much liked to have met him and argued with him, but he was killed during the 2008 war when the Israeli army bombarded a municipal building in Gaza where he happened to be at the time. I knew him a little, I used to listen to his sermons when I was teaching at the mosque. He had an open mind. In fact there were a lot of open-minded and discerning people like him, except that when Hamas assumed power their minds closed up.

That letter became a borderline in my life, a watershed between Asmaa before and Asmaa after. It set up a permanent state of defiance between my uncle and me—he with his military power and the fear that it inspires and me with my pen. My foreign connections and the support of various human rights associations created a certain balance of power between us. It drove him mad. I started to become well-known: people who were facing difficulties would come to see me so that I would make their problems public. Every time I introduced myself people asked, "Are you related to Saïd al-Ghoul?" I'm sure people asked him the same question regarding me. Thus it was that we became the two celebrities of the family: he for his harshness, I for my freedom.

I wrote to Sohaib to tell him about all the aggravation caused by the letter he helped me to write. He replied, "You really are crazy," and suggested we see each other again, which we did. When I went to Seoul to work in the restaurant on the weekend we would meet near to the Eiti Won district where he lived. We would talk until the morning. He was the complete opposite of me: as much as he had adopted Western habits—I used to run into him with Korean or Chinese girls—on the intellectual level he had remained a staunch Muslim, the son of a famous Islamic opponent of the regime in Morocco. We argued all the time, we didn't agree on anything, neither on religion nor on morality nor on general behavior. He had done a master's degree in economics in Paris and in Korea was working toward a degree in Communication Studies. He was an intelligent man but completely submissive in questions of religion. He was another who told me about sufferings of the grave and promised that I would end up in hell. Suddenly, right in the middle of an argument, we fell in love: I discovered that I loved him and it was the same on his side. For all that we didn't sit down to say "we're in love" but to fight it out over anything and everything. We would throw in each others' faces comments such as "Why are you telling me this?" "And you, why are you still smoking cigarettes?" and all that in literary Arabic in the depths of Korea.

In reality he loved me and detested me at the same time. We fasted together during Ramadan, that was wonderful.

But even if my mind was much more liberal than his, my attitudes remained Middle-Eastern. We said to ourselves, "Why shouldn't we get married? We could go to Spain and live together." He contacted my father who was in agreement as soon as he heard that he knew the Koran by heart. But my mother was violently opposed to the idea: "Have you gone mad? You're going to abandon your child to go and live in Spain? An Egyptian wasn't enough for you, you're bringing home a Moroccan to us now?" I realized she was right. I very much liked Sohaib's way of thinking, his cast of mind, but that's not enough for a marriage. It was more sensible to separate.

One night I had a dream. I was with my Grandfather Jomaa beside a waterfall and my father said, "Your grandfather's going to die." He died two weeks later. I started crying, I fell ill. Sohaib came out from Seoul in a taxi and found all my writer friends at my bedside: my South-African friend Ketso, an Indian poet called Anbar Ali, Leon, a Mexican writer and also an Argentine whose name I've forgotten. I was crying all the time; they prepared a meal for me and stayed in my bedroom until I fell asleep. But with Sohaib it was truly all over. Later, when I was better, I started writing letters to him that I pinned to the door of his apartment in Seoul. His reply would be, "I've received your letter," without further comment. At the point when I was leaving Korea, in 2008, I felt that I was still in love with him. I asked him whether he didn't want to go with me, we could get married in Egypt. He didn't want to. In Gaza I started my computer and discovered a long email he'd sent me: "The sun set after you left. I will not see it again in Korea."

17

The Woman with the Beauty Spot

A MONG THE MEMORIES I brought back home is a meeting with our national poet, Mahmoud Darwish. He was the guest of honor at a festival of Asian literature, a large-scale event organized in a town outside Seoul. I had only just arrived when I saw him in the hotel lobby with two female translators, who were translating from Korean into Arabic for him. I dropped my suitcases and went over to introduce myself. He asked in slightly sharp tones, "What brings you here?" I didn't dare admit that I had been invited as a writer, I told him I was a journalist. I knew that he was cold and wary towards people he didn't know, especially young girls who swarmed around him—how could he have known that I wasn't like that? I also knew that he didn't like Gaza very much. In his books he called it, "The land of strength and despair." The next day I ran into him in the lobby again. He didn't look very well. He called out to me, "What is it with these Koreans? I can't stand their food. They don't give you any choice."

"What do you want?"

"I want to get out of here."

"Okay, but on the condition you let me be your tour guide."

He could leave the festival because he had appeared in the opening session and thus fulfilled his obligations... We set out with the two friends who were accompanying him.

The festival had reserved hotel rooms for us in Seoul. When they gave us our keys, he asked, "How is it that your room is next to mine while the others are on a different floor?" I told him I had no idea but I could see he didn't believe me. Despite that, we became friends. We went out every day, we looked for the restaurants serving the best non-Korean food, we walked... I talked to him about Gaza and Hamas, about which he didn't know very much. He told me he'd read the short stories in my first collection and gave me a copy of *Memory for Forgetfulness*, his book about the 1982 siege of Beirut, with a nice dedication. He talked about the young Arabs who criticized him, calling him the "poet of the powers" because he had written some speeches for Arafat before renouncing him. One evening when we were walking in the dark together, I asked him, "Is Seoul not the most beautiful city in the world?" He said, "No, the most beautiful one is Paris."

He had a bad back and I found a masseuse for him. One hour later in the lobby, one of his accompanying friends asked him what it had been like, and he said, "Very odd. She was old and blind. She massaged me as if there was no problem, she used the telephone as a matter of course. How could she see the number of my room?"

We checked—the numbers on the door were not in relief. That mystery has never been solved. I made fun of him. "You come to this country full of young, beautiful Korean girls and all you get is an old, blind woman?" He shrugged his shoulders and said, "You see?"

At night there was just a thin wall between us. In the morning I said, "I heard you coughing."

"How did you manage that?"

"The wall's not that thick."

"So why didn't I hear you?"

He told me the story of an American billionaire who

loved himself so much that he kept his poop in receptacles and refused to throw it away. He took everything lightly, was always making jokes. I wanted to take him to a flower festival—the Koreans work wonders with flowers, transforming them into all sorts of things. On the way there, the traffic jams irritated him: "Who told you I wanted to go to a festival? I don't want to go anywhere!" I remained silent. Then I told him that in our schools they studied his famous poem *Write down: I am an Arab*. He burst out, "I don't like that poem! It's enclosed me in a frame that I reject. I'm not like that! I don't bear all that suffering, all that sorrow on my shoulders!" We finally arrived at the festival and walked around the stands. All at once he was amazed and said, "I must thank you... and apologize."

Write down: I am an Arab is a proud affirmation of identity as a reaction to the humiliations and suffering. All Palestinians are proud of that poem—except the poet who wrote it because he very quickly sensed that there was something other than the militant position to express, something less clear and more difficult. When he starts out, a poet doesn't define the identity of his poetry in advance, he doesn't know where he is going to end up—how could he? Mahmoud Darwish started out as a patriotic, nationalist poet, embracing the cause of Palestine. Later on it became clear that his identity was more generally humanistic. He even wrote about the American Indians. Those who criticize him say that he has changed his position, notably with regard to Israel. I don't believe that at all. He simply came to understand the extent to which poetry and literature are more important than everything else. Why should they carry a message serving a nation, a country, a village or a family? When he was asked what peace was, Mahmoud Darwish replied, "Peace is planting the garden behind my house and loving the woman with the beauty spot." His aim was not necessarily to throw stones at the occupier.

In my blog, the things that happened to me or that I imagined, the events in political life and in my private (or indeed fantasy) life naturally blended in with what I considered literary texts. I put a lot of myself into them. But journalism has left its mark on it, imposing its scrupulous respect for the facts, and it has slightly ruined their delicate construction. I have given up my blog, I've stopped composing poems, I don't write short stories anymore—even if I haven't entirely abandoned the genre. I know that there is something at work inside me. All the time. There is not one moment in which my mind stops working or closes down.

I told Mahmoud that two months ago I'd met a French writer in Korea who had talked about him—Le Clézio.

"It was at a literary colloquium. I saw this tall, handsome man coming over to me, he introduced himself, I didn't know his name nor that he was famous, I had only noticed the attention he was attracting. He was very elegant. He talked about the island where he lived, about you, Mahmoud, whom he'd met, his love for Palestine... I told him about the contradiction between my life in Gaza and my life abroad and how I felt I had two different personalities. He asked me, "How do you mean?" and I explained. He couldn't stop asking me questions about my split personality.

"I'm sure he was looking for characters for his next novel."

We laughed. When we left, we stayed without moving for a long time before we said goodbye. The next day I sent him a message to make sure that he had arrived safely on the West Bank. After he died I heard that he'd been looking for my telephone number to call me—just to say hello. He couldn't find it and I, obviously, didn't dare telephone him. He died just like that. I was deeply moved.

18

Your Religion Comes Before Your Land

WHEN I GOT BACK from Korea I stayed in Egypt to see how the situation was going to turn out for me after the business with the letter. I spent two months there. During that time my father asked a relatively open Hamas member of parliament to try to mediate. He received a favorable reply, and I could return to Gaza. Two or three days later I saw a white vehicle, a jeep, waiting outside our house. It suddenly drove off, almost knocking me over. I threw myself down behind a tree. It was like a message to frighten me and put me on my guard. After that incident, nothing else happened.

I was happy with life after my return, I had missed the country so much. Because of the letter my parents had been boycotted by their close relatives but outside the family their popularity had very much increased, just as mine had because I had defended the law, which doesn't happen that often in Gaza. I took up my work again with *Al Ayyam*, saw my friends, walked bareheaded around the streets, nothing had changed. I hardly noticed that for the first time I was living under the regime of Hamas, with my uncle still responsible for security in Rafah. I had seen that people in America and Korea exhausted themselves in their work and hardly saw their children at all. I told myself that things were a thousand times better in Gaza, and not only for me, for everyone. Outsiders who come to spend two weeks there end up staying for six months: the territory possesses some kind of magic. You can become yourself there, you sense the value of your own life, and the fact that you're a Muslim, a Christian or a Jew has nothing to do with that. It's not the Kaaba in Mecca that's the centre of the world, as the Saudis maintain, but Gaza, the land of Sampson and Delilah.

It wasn't long before I was being pestered again by the Islamists and the sheikhs who legislate women's condition, our way of life, our freedoms—while they know nothing about them. In a general way, political Islam establishes a separation between life and religion while at the same time accusing the secularism, which it detests, of making a separation between religion and the state. It is the Islamists who are the divisive force because they translate everything into prohibitions. If you respected their precepts it would mean that you never went out, abstained from watching TV and spent all your time reading the Koran. Basically: doing nothing but wait for the Last Day.

During the 1970s, the period of the Palestinian left wing and the Popular Front, the duty of a militant was *not* to die but to preserve his life for the land, the country, the worldwide revolution, the end of the exploitation of men by men and whatever. Under Islamist rule people learn to love death—and, like it or not, a woman who loses her son starts believing he's gone to Paradise, otherwise he'd have died for nothing. She needs that lie to be able to cope with her loss. Fatah is a populist party with no specific ideology, which is why anyone can identify with it. But for Hamas there is a clear division between those who pray and those who don't, Muslims and Christians, Sunnis and Shiites. You haven't liberated your country because you've fought well but because you're a Muslim and have said your prayers. The typical member of Hamas is a Sunni Muslim who gets up at dawn to go to the mosque and criticizes his neighbor because he doesn't belong to Hamas. "Religion comes before the land," that is the principle. As one of the principal leaders of the movement, Mahmoud al Zahar, put it in an interview, "The *Ummah Islamiya* (the Islamic nation) includes many nationalities such as the Malays, the Bengalis, the Chinese, the Arabs, the Persians as well as the Turks, the Berbers, and the Africans." During the time of Nasser you could be a Muslim, a Christian, a Druze or even a Jew, everyone was united by the fact of being an Arab, at least in theory. But Hamas rejects Arab nationalism and detests Nasser. With them you can be French, Pakistani, Afghan or South African—as long as you're a Sunni Muslim, it's okay. Fortunately my father had taught me another idea of religion when I was little: "Islam is every believer who gives his heart to God."

My criticisms of Hamas in *Al Ayyam* were less theoretical. For example, I told how the Islamist movement had forbidden the "feast of love," St. Valentines' Day, by prohibiting presents that were red or wrapped up in red, as was the tradition. Hamas' men had gone around to the shops— "Don't sell anything red," and the traders had obeyed. I talked about this with a woman who was doing her shopping. She said, "You can love your father and your mother without needing this feast of love."

"Yes, but whatever it is that makes it possible to love your father or your mother is precisely what allows you to love the son of your neighbor."

"No."

"Why not?"

"Because St. Valentine's Day is a feast of the unbelievers."

"But this feast existed even before religion. It's purpose was to marry lovers, not to encourage them to get into bad ways."

She had no reply to that—which I put in my article. I was accused of being permissive, of encouraging relationships between boys and girls, of advocating the equality of the sexes. My father had taught me to say, "Us human beings," rather than, "Us women," which is the reason why I've never claimed to be a feminist. But in the Palestinian feminist organization that had just recruited me, I discovered that my colleagues weren't really feminist. Above all they were afraid that Hamas might close down their institution and they would lose their salary. When the Islamic powers forbade women to smoke a hookah in public, they didn't dare even to issue a communiqué. None of them said, "I'm going to smoke a hookah in a café because no one has the right to forbid me to do so." None of them went to make a declaration on television. And when the international media came to ask us about it, they replied that it was a sensitive subject and they preferred not to discuss it. So the journalists came to me—no one else dared to declare that it was an intolerable sexist measure.

In the aftermath of this, I suggested that my organization should initiate a research project—based on sheikhs and Islamic scholars attracted by modernity—to establish that Islam itself was not opposed to the rights of women. What a suggestion I'd made! "Are you out of your mind? Do you want the whole of society to rise up against us?" And they were the ones who told me that—the feminists of Gaza who, financed by the European Union, Sweden and Switzerland, had never gone out into the field before 2012 and did nothing more than draw up reports.

The director took me to one side and said, "You're seen with your men friends in the cafés too often. You're working for us at the moment, you represent us. Try to go there less so that people don't badmouth our institution. As for me, I'm prepared to cover my head and tell everyone that I'm veiled in order to promote women's rights." And she was seen as one of the main feminists of Gaza! These women had appointed me and paid me a royal salary of $800 a month because they needed a known face that could be shown while most of them were veiled. They came to the office to make something to eat—quick-cooking Asian noodles—and to malign each other. I understood how Hamas in power could intimidate people and force them to betray themselves without even having to lift a hand. Eventually I resigned.

19

A Shameless Hussy?

A NYONE COMING TO GAZA will see at once how complicated our society is. It's not just a matter of the political power, it's society as a whole that is immersed in an atmosphere which is horrible for women. During the time when Fatah was in control, I stopped a policeman in the street to complain about a man who made a sexist remark because of the way I was dressed. He looked me up and down before saying, "The man's right, you're beautiful dressed like that."

It was hardly any better with Hamas. I went to the police station with my lawyer to report the threats that had been made on my blog. The captain asked me, "What threats?"

"I've been called a whore."

"How do you dare use words like that with me?"

"I'm simply repeating the words of the threat that was made," I said, showing the email that I'd printed out.

My lawyer broke in, "What business is that of yours? It is your duty to record the complaint, that's all."

He acquiesced. When we went back to see him the next day, he said to me, "I've read your blog. It's very good but you're too bold."

A police captain! I was pleased that he'd read it. He added, "There are, however, things you shouldn't write."

"What, for example?"

"You say that during one of your trips you found yourself without anywhere to sleep one night. So you went to see a man friend in a university residence hall and he gave you his waterbed for the night."

"And what's wrong with that? Such things happen to everyone on their travels, we're ready to sleep anywhere because we don't have enough money, though most people keep quiet about it and lie."

He said nothing. But my complaint was never recorded. During those days, if a father saw his daughter talking to a man, he could kill her, and so could her brother. I wrote an article about a girl who had suffered that fate because her father had caught their neighbor's son jumping out of her window at three in the morning. The father hit the boy before throwing him in some alley, but he didn't die. The girl did. Among the neighbors, the murder is accepted, it's nothing. They stand out in the street by their doors, laughing and chatting, passing the time as if nothing had happened, as if there wasn't a girl who'd just been murdered. Men, of course. It was only the mother who was sick about it and the victim's brothers and sisters as well. The father will go to prison but not for long, less than three years. That's the law: "in cases of legitimate defense or defense of honor, the sentence will be reduced"—and it wasn't Hamas that introduced that law, it was Fatah! Don't think that one is more progressive than the other. As soon as women are concerned, the pair of them agree. In 2014, fourteen young women were killed on the West Bank and in Gaza. Has anyone been punished for these crimes? Most of the young women murdered in those so-called "crimes of honor" were virgins. It's enough to make you cry.

One day my brother Yasser saw a girl in the apartment opposite, she was absolutely superb, as beautiful as an angel, blond hair, blue eyes, a true princess. He found out that she often came to see her grandmother, whose windows were opposite ours. That was how they came to see each other and they started to talk using the interphone of the apartment block. The girl's uncle caught them using this ploy and told her father, who suddenly turned up at our place. I knew that he was a member of Fatah and had the reputation of being quite a hard man. He asked to speak to my father; my sisters and I listened at the door:

"My daughter, I've hit her, I've given her a good thrashing, I've locked her up."

"Why?" Papa replied, "Nothing wrong's happened, they're very young."

I went into the parlor and headed straight for Imane's father. "Listen, you're like my uncle... I've been in love, my father's been in love and I'm sure you've been in love too. Why are you trying to forbid something so natural?"

These words had the effect of calming the guy down. He replied that he wasn't a reactionary, he could understand, there was no need to defend his daughter's honor from people like us. My father broke in, "I'll come to see you tomorrow to ask for the hand of your daughter for my son."

They shook hands on it and Imane's father went out, satisfied. My parents went to see him the next day, but in the meantime he'd changed his mind. "Imane has been promised to a cousin in Saudi Arabia..." She stopped going to see her grandmother. Yasser was hard hit but stood up to it, "It's over, I'm going to forget her." The young woman started calling me, "I'm suffocating, I can't go on anymore, I'd like to continue my education, go to college but Papa wants to marry me off..." What could I do? Her father had effectively engaged her to the cousin in question and she vanished from our life.

Two years later, at the time of the breaking of the Ramadan fast, I was sitting there quietly after having eaten and I heard my mother and sisters whispering. Among the words that came to me I could make out, "Imane is dead." I cried out, "What?!" They hadn't wanted Yasser and me to hear about it but now they had to tell us what they knew. Imane had fought with her father because she wanted to go to college, he had put her under all sorts of pressure without being able to make her change her mind. To punish her, he'd locked her in the bathroom where she'd swallowed some poison for cockroaches. They'd taken her to the hospital with her stomach all swollen... The doctors were unable to save her, she'd managed to commit suicide." I saw red. "Suicide? You're lying! It's her father who killed her."

I don't know how, but I found myself out in the street, Yasser running in front of me. We got to Imane's house. The first thing we saw was her father carried by two men and crying. I ran up to him.

"What's happened, uncle?"

"Imane's dead, Asmaa."

"And you're the cause! It was you all! You killed Imane!"

And I exploded, it was over, I couldn't stand this horror anymore. The women dragged me into a room and tried to justify themselves.

"God knows, it wasn't us who killed her."

"You're all just lying. It was you!"

"No it wasn't! Imane was preparing the meal for the breaking of the fast and she mistook the cockroach poison for hummus..."

"Are you kidding me? How could she have eaten if she was still fasting?"

"It was because she was having her period, she wasn't obliged to fast..."

Another aunt arrived and told me that Imane had confused the poison with pepper. I was furious. At that moment one of Imane's friends arrived and we stayed there crying together: "Imane, as beautiful as an angel... You'd say she'd come down to Earth in order to die... A *houri*[3]... That was why her father was so jealous!"

Just as we were leaving, one of Imane's uncles took Yasser by the arm. "Go to her grave," he said, "and sing her the songs she loved."

I couldn't believe my ears. Suddenly they were no longer ashamed of love that had become *halal* now that Imane was dead!

I spoke out against the family throughout the district. I wrote up her story, a friend helped me to translate it into English and I sent it to a European newspaper... that never published it. Imane was sixteen. Yasser went to her grave, he showed me the photos. I told him, "Forget her, Yasser. Get married, take the apartment I'm living in," but he refused. He said nothing, he played soccer, busied himself repairing computers, that's what he loved doing.

I regretted not having listened more closely to Imane when she telephoned me, but I do have to admit that the Hamas people in power didn't simply turn a blind eye. They arrested the father in order to find out whether he'd killed her or not. In fact he hadn't, she really had committed suicide. But why? Strange as it may seem, Hamas punishes so-called crimes of honor much more than Fatah. They see to it that any father or brother who kills his daughter or his sister stays in prison. Hamas has also set up a 'safe house' where young women who are threatened, or pregnant without being married, can find refuge. Fatah never did that. Girls who go to the police can spend a few nights there— which didn't stop them from sometimes being pestered by the policemen. When they come out they are returned to their parents who can kill them immediately. Hamas goes to

3 *houri*: a virgin in Paradise promised to believers

great lengths to explain the extent to which love outside marriage is *haram* but ultimately they do try to protect girls from murder!

The truth is that there is a profound correlation between 'resistance' and 'honor'. The 'depraved' morals introduced by the occupiers are indeed seen as a permanent source of corruption for our society which, as everyone knows, is 'decent, moral and God-fearing.' The harsher the occupation is, the more resistance to the occupation expresses itself in a pathological hardening of attitudes in the matter of 'honor'. There has been terrible repression carried out in its name: the PLO, Fatah, the Popular Front, Hamas, they've all been at it. Resistance and honor are a regression which always means: the oppression of women. It's on the West Bank that they resort to weapons most often, where they kill the most women. If it hadn't been for the occupation, Gaza might have been a seaside tourist destination.

After my return from Korea I worked and wrote without worrying about anything. The first threat I received 'as a woman' came from one of the officials of the Ministry of Information. "You are pretty and divorced, so watch out..." Put simply, that meant he was preparing to attack my reputation by any means whatever. It kept me awake at night. The local shopkeeper, a decent guy, warned me that 'people from Security' had been asking him for information about me—when did I go out, when did I come home, whom did I see, etc. In every district there is someone, generally a member of Hamas, who has the task of providing information on the people who live in his area. He's called the *Zannane*: the man who makes zzzz around you, who sees you though you don't see him—it's also what we call the Israeli drones. I immediately moved. A friend from the Popular Front helped me find an apartment in an out-of-the-way district; I also stopped going to the newspaper offices, and they lost track of me.

It was at that point, in August 2008, that Mahmoud Darwish died. I was devastated when I heard the news. A cultural organization, the Kattan Foundation, which had awarded me a prize, asked me if I'd write an article on him, but I didn't have the heart. I just wanted to go and hide in the apartment, which I'd rented to escape from Hamas, and stay put. My parents came to see me there—they started to cry because they couldn't do anything for me, there was no one to protect me, no one to act as intermediary and allow me to take up my life again without worrying. I did, though, eventually manage to write the article on Mahmoud Darwish. I told how happy we'd been together in Korea, how we'd laughed and how we'd argued. For me he was neither a poet nor a genius, nor an elegant man but a wonderful person, simply a person.

Then suddenly I was fed up with all of this. I decided to face the situation without worrying about possible rumors, and I went back to live with my parents. Later on, when Hamas threw me in prison and heaped abuse on me, they discovered that they had nothing against me that 'stuck', I'd been maligned. Those who'd bet that I was a 'shameless hussy' had lost.

I came out of there exhausted. Many of my friends had decided to leave the country. They expected that the powers-that-be would attack wider society and preferred to take evasive action. One had opted for Spain, another for Norway, a third for Sweden. I let myself be persuaded as well. Eventually there were ten of us who got our visas and one-way tickets for some other country. I withdrew at the last moment. They all went and I stayed behind, along with a dear friend, a man who had also decided that you shouldn't leave Gaza like that. The two of us found ourselves somewhat alone but feeling what we had done was right. We continued to struggle within society and to get annoyed with a lot of people. Later that friend set up an institution, and that obliged him to keep his mouth shut: he could no longer criticize Hamas. That's the way things are. All those who reach a certain position are supposed to monitor themselves, make concessions and ultimately become like everyone else. I had no association, no position, no money. I had to forgo some particular things in order to be able to continue and I gave up a lot, but with no regrets.

20

War

BEFORE HANGING UP, I said to my friend at the other end of the line, "I'll get dressed and come and meet you." It was 11:24 on December 27, 2008. I stood up, the explosions began before I was on my feet, the infernal rhythm, the deafening, rolling sound of shellfire, my mother ran out onto the balcony, screaming the names of her three daughters, who were at school, the balconies of the surrounding apartments echoing her cries. No advance indication, no preliminaries, the whole town just suddenly started trembling. Our crazy neighbor, called Israel, had opened fire on Gaza without warning. War. Forgetting I was dressed the way I am when I'm staying at home, I charged out into the street, distraught. My mother, on the balcony, was leaning so far over I thought she was going to fall. My brother Yasser also burst out into the street, he jumped in front of me like a gazelle and dashed off to my sisters' school to get there before anything happened. Their school was beside the Arafat police station, my son's close to the headquarters of Fatah Security and a fifteen-story tower-block with official offices, both possible targets of the intensive bombardment. Gasping for breath, I ran on, worried stiff. Before I got there I knew that the tower-block in question had been flattened by a bomb dropped by an airplane and that the Security headquarters had been destroyed by another bomb. It was just at the moment when the schools were out. In Gaza the educational establishments run by UNRWA have two sessions: the first finishes at 11:15, the second begins at 11:30. It's precisely between the two, at the moment when the children are passing each other, that the bombardment started—which explains the great number of victims. On my way, I passed women who were crying, people slapping their heads, ambulances with sirens screaming... I ran until a driver, who was hurrying to collect his children, stopped and gave me a lift. He dropped me off outside the school, all the windows in the district were shattered. In the yard the children were wailing, terrified. Oh my God, where's my son? I ran up the stairs to his class-room. His chair, empty, was covered in pieces of broken glass, huge shards. "Where's Nasser? Where's Nasser?" I cried. No one answered. There was no blood on the chair. Then suddenly I heard a little voice, "Mama!" It was him who found me. His face was bright red with fear, he hadn't cried, it would have been a thousand times better if he had. I took him in my arms and started to calm him down. Parents, worried out of their minds, were arriving one after another to collect their children. Nasser was still silent, dazed. We went out to see if we could find a car. At the school gate he finally opened his lips, "Is it Hamas, Mama?" and I said, "No, it's the Israeli army."

We took advantage of a lull in the bombardment to get home. We found my sisters there, all in tears. Yasser had brought them home, terrified. From that moment on, all the family except for me, who had to go out to work, stayed in the apartment for the twenty-two days of almost uninterrupted bombardment, twenty-two days of terror. Every day they changed the room where they slept—"That room's better protected,"—"No, that other one's safer,"—according to complicated calculations based on the axis of the shells and the greater or lesser proximity of potential targets. Neighbors from all around came to spend the night in our two-story apartment block which was thought to be less exposed, squeezing together in our stairwell. That was daily life during the war of 2008, called "Operation Cast Lead."

So I was going out every day to provide articles for *Al Ayyam*, but also for another paper, *Al Quds al Arabi* and a center for the defense of the freedom of the press, *Skeyes*, founded in memory of a famous Lebanese journalist, Samir Kassir, who had been assassinated. Moroccan television also called on my services, I was working twenty-four hours a day, which meant I had to sleep at the office. I wasn't afraid during that war—except of Hamas' men. No one went out except journalists, so that when they saw people walking in the night they would ask, in terrifying tones, "Where are you coming from? What are you doing?"—because collaborators also generally went out at night. Sometimes Yasser would accompany me, thus exposing himself to questions charged with suspicion. My mother said, "Get one of your male colleagues from the paper to accompany you, your brother's been arrested twice already." I had to get there whatever happened. In the empty streets I heard nothing but the insistent throb of the Israeli drones—the zzzz—that filled the sky and saw everything. The electricity was cut off, I couldn't even see my own hand. I only managed to find my bearings because I knew the way: total darkness and the risk of dying at any moment.

I have never really understood what set this war off. Six months previously Mubarak's Egypt had helped to negotiate a truce between Israel and Hamas, which provided for a lifting of the blockade of Gaza and a cessation of the launching of rockets into Israeli territory. The launching of rockets had never completely ceased and the blockade had never been lifted, but the truce had been entirely respected for several long months before the confrontations began again. Only a few days before it broke out, the Hamas government claimed that Egypt had given them assurance that there would be no war. In this belief they had gone ahead with the ceremony of handing out diplomas at the police college and the first shell had exploded right in the middle of it. According to Hamas, the police lost two hundred and thirty officers during the war, one of them a general.

Taken by surprise, the leaders of Gaza decided despite everything to appear on TV to make a public declaration. But some channels refused to take them on the pretext that the Israeli army had threatened reprisals if they invited the 'terrorists' to their studios. Balmedia, a small company that hosted a certain number of channels, decided to take the risk. It occupied two separate areas at the top of a tower-block. The moment the representatives of the Islamist power entered the first, all the Balmedia personnel ran to take shelter in the other—the Israeli helicopters were circling around the tower at that very moment. I stayed there, sitting a few meters away from where the representatives of Hamas were. One of them came over to me.

"Go and take cover with the others," he said.

"No. If you have to die, I'll die with you. We're in the same situation faced with the occupation."

I put on a proud face, but deep down inside I was scared stiff, quivering like a leaf. In the studio there were only the controller of the channel, the cameraman and me. The Israelis knew where the Hamas leaders were, of course, they could probably see them live. If they decided to launch a 'personal' missile of the type that goes in through the window, everything in the room would have been destroyed in one second. The communiqué read out to the camera by the Hamas representatives was naturally very tough: "We will face up to it, we will resist, etc.," contrary to the real situation—we were sitting there wetting our pants. The missiles didn't appear and the recording was finished with no harm done.

Al Shorouk Tower, where I spent that night and where many journalists were working, was bombarded a few minutes after I left. Almost at the same moment the Palestine Tower, which housed the offices of *Al Ayyam*, was also hit, as well as the luxurious assembly and wedding rooms by the sea that belonged to Hamas. One of my brothers went out onto the balcony to assess the damage to the Daoud Tower, opposite where we lived, and was hit by two little splinters, nothing serious, a bit of blood. When I arrived home I found my mother bandaging his wound, my son in tears and my father, who wasn't very happy with the situation. Looking out of the window I felt as if I was in a reconstruction of a scene from 1948 which I hadn't lived through: thousands of refugees loaded with bundles, rolled-up mattresses and children in tears were coming toward us. My father said, "Let's do the same as them. Let's take refuge in a school," but my mother replied in no uncertain terms, "We're not moving from our apartment!"

The Israeli army was coming closer at every moment, it was perhaps going to enter Tel el Hawa, our district. My parents didn't know what to do, I was wondering what the best solution would be, we argued, the bombardment continued, we looked after my brother, my son was crying... and I had work to do. Since there was neither electricity nor Internet at home, I quickly came to a decision: leaving the others where they were, I picked up Nasser and took him to the office with me. Once there he watched, with disarming curiosity, the advance of the Israeli tanks we could see in the distance. I was afraid for my son while he, because I was with him, wasn't afraid at all.

As the war continued there was a rumor going around that Hamas was taking advantage of the situation to quietly liquidate the members of Fatah that were in their way. This rumor was to be confirmed later in Judge Goldstone's report for the United Nations that condemned both Israel and Hamas—before what it had said about Israel's crimes were withdrawn, provoking an official protest from the other three members of the commission. But during the war, no one had any need of that report to believe in the reality of the vendetta launched by Hamas. This campaign of assassinations was to be there in black and white in the Goldstone Report which cited eye-witnesses in support of its allegations. Subsequently Hamas came down on those witnesses as well as the human rights organizations who had helped collect the information. These lamentable reprisals could, of course, do nothing to cast doubt on the truth of the facts established by the report; on the contrary, they confirmed them.

The war finished on January 18, 2009, the day after my birthday. My mother laughed. She lit a candle on a tin of sardines, opened to celebrate the occasion, and I blew it out.

21

Feelings of Anger

ONCE THE WAR WAS OVER, all the accumulated fury at the men of Hamas in power came out. They were accused of nothing less than having left the people in the lurch: there had been no protection, no emergency services— while the movement's leaders for their part were well hidden. Even greater was the anger at Israel, whose operation had caused the death of more than 1400 people. This anger was of a different kind—you can't hold a grudge against the enemy in the same way as you can against those who were supposed to protect you.

In Al Hilal Hospital I came across the survivors of the Samuni family, 21 members of which had been killed in the house where the Israeli army had gathered them together two days previously. They thought they were safe, they were all in the interior courtyard, baking bread on a traditional oven, when the shell came down right in the middle of them and tore them to pieces. One of the boys told me that he had spent three days among the bodies of his family, watching the hens and cats come and eat them. With his grandmother and two other escapees he had survived on uncooked rice and rotten tomatoes. It was only after three days that the army lifted for a few hours the checkpoints that were stopping the emergency services from getting through. The Palestinian media were full of this crime, which the United

Nations was to regard as "the most serious" thing that happened during "Operation Cast Lead"—but the Israeli military judges found nothing to justify taking legal action against those responsible.

Furious with Hamas, disgusted at the impunity enjoyed by Israel, suffocating from a kind of impotent anger, how could the Gazans react? By turning against themselves! They directed the futile rage they felt on those around them, throwing horrible accusations at each other, harming each other, getting divorced. A general regression! My brother Mustafa criticized the Islamist government; my father didn't agree, he thought it wasn't the right time to attack Hamas, we had to stay united at all costs. My mother took Mustafa's side, my father lost his temper, packed a few things and went to live in our house in Rafah. We tried to get him to come back, we begged him, my son was distressed because he was very attached to him... All to no avail, so we accepted the situation, we turned inward and stopped asking about him. It was over. We had to become stronger, start something new. We weren't the only ones, the war had torn everyone apart, not a single family had been spared. My father came to Gaza every day for his work at the university without ever coming to see us. We knew that he wasn't exactly delighted with living in Rafah, he stayed there out of obstinacy. He lived there all alone for almost a whole year.

That started me questioning my own attitude as a mother; I was aware that I had failed in my duty to my son. I couldn't stand his father and I got divorced without thinking about him, I traveled in search of myself and once the Iraqi psychiatrist told me to distance myself from the situation, I handed him over to my parents so that I could get away. I can't even remember the day when he took his first steps. I started to cry at the thought of what I'd done to him: my suffering and the shock of the divorce had even weakened my attachment to my son. My father was always saying to me, "You're a mother in your heart, not in your mind." The crisis made me see that I hadn't really taken proper care of Nasser nor concerned myself with him.

War isn't something that goes away, it stays there inside your body. We were invited to a wedding. Half an hour before leaving my mother put her hand over her heart and said, "Asmaa, I have a pain in my chest."

I was worried, she reassured me, "Go and have your bath, it'll be all right."

I could see that she was in a bad way. She was having a heart attack. The shock of the war had broken hearts. I called my father. He was still sulking but he came from the university hospital straight away. My mother was admitted to the intensive care ward and her heart calmed down. I stayed close to her, which isn't allowed in that ward and when I refused to leave, the hospital called the police! I had to go down to the ground floor but I didn't leave the building. I spent the night walking around and around, in the cold, outside the shack for the Hamas armed guards. I talked to them for the first time since the war. One of them was a decent guy. He allowed me to stay in the nurses' office, which I regularly sneaked out of to go upstairs and see how Mama was doing.

One day in January 2009, I was standing on a roof with my cameraman filming for Moroccan television the funeral of Nizar Rayan, a Hamas leader who had been killed by a missile with his wife and four children. Suddenly cries of "Allahu Akbar!" came from the people we could see crowding together. They had just found the body of one of the daughters under the ruins. It was brought out while the camera was still rolling. We finished our work, got our things together and left. I was wearing wide trousers, a long-sleeved blouse with, over it, a shawl that came down to my waist; as usual my hair was uncovered.

An orange and white ambulance came toward us. The driver, a bearded man wearing the stretcher-bearers' uniform, shouted out of the window, "Cover your hair." I replied, "I don't want to," and continued on my way. The ambulance screeched to a halt and the man got out. I realized he was a religious fanatic. He strode toward me, clearly determined to hit me. The cameraman stood in his way. The man shouted, "You have no shame! You don't know God."

I shouted even louder, "God doesn't belong to you. I know God better than you. I'm working here."

I don't know where I got the strength for that from. The cameraman grabbed my shawl and covered my head. I pushed him away violently. "Don't interfere! Leave me in peace! This gentleman should get on with his own business!"

A clean-shaven man came up and caught the bearded man by the arm. "What's gotten into you, are you out of your senses? She's showing the world what's happening to us and you're taking her to account because she's bareheaded?" He pushed my aggressor into a car and took him away.

I was still angry with my cameraman. "You're a cretin who has no idea about anything! You're supposed to stay beside me rather than trying to cover my head. We're stuck in the shit here and my hair's a problem?" We got back to the office and I still hadn't finished bawling him out. When he heard what had happened the director supported me. I couldn't have acted differently. It was more fitting for me to be hit than to have my hair covered against my will.

I found it impossible to accept the regression that the war and its frustrations were starting to impose. Refusing the veil—I can't even say that was my freedom, it was rather my refusal to be two-faced. One day I said to a woman who scolded me for wearing trousers in a mosque, "God would accept my prayer even if I prayed bareheaded." I find this claim to the right to make others cover themselves truly intolerable. The self-righteous want to interfere with your feelings about God, right down to your relations with Him. In such conditions even to feel the presence of God is difficult. I could, of course, still be myself even if I covered my head, but why should I do that? If women want to use the veil to affirm their identity, then let them go ahead. I feel no inclination to emphasize my religious identity, I simply want to be myself.

When you're swimming against the tide, you sometimes feel alone. But *Behind the Scenes in the War*, a series I made to talk about the upheavals the conflict had caused in our daily lives, finally won the very prestigious Dubai Press Club prize for journalism. And Human Rights Watch awarded me a Hellman/Hammet grant of $4,000, intended to "support writers who have been persecuted for having expressed opinions contrary to those of their government." I felt that the people I'd been talking about day after day—the ordinary folk who'd been crushed and forgotten—had suddenly been given recognition.

22

The Beach Affair

IT WAS IN THE MONTH of June, and my friend May and I were sitting on the sand, in jeans and shirts, chatting. The beach cafeteria belongs to her father—that day there were plenty of customers. We went for a swim, in our clothes. After we'd been bathing we noticed a guy in plain clothes who was vaguely hanging around us, but we didn't pay much attention to him. I wanted to get changed because my clothes were too wet but there was no closed room, just two tiny cubicles, one of which was used as a toilet, the other to make tea and coffee. I knew that one of the nearby beach huts was being used by Taher, a colleague from *Al Ayyam*, his wife and ten children. I called him, "I'd like to come and get changed in your beach hut," and he said there was no problem. Night was falling, and May asked her young brother to go with me. When we got there Taher showed me the bathroom where I could be alone. May's brother waited for me. When I came out again, I saw four bearded men by the hut. As soon as they saw me they came to ask for my passport.

"Why? What's the problem?'

"We want to see your passport," one of them replied, "that's all."

I asked Taher what was going on; the bearded man broke in, "What were you doing on the beach?'

"What were we doing? We were sitting there in the

middle of all the people, we've nothing to hide. I came here to get changed. This is my colleague Taher, from the *Al Ayyam* newspaper, his wife, his children and the brother of my friend who accompanied me here. What is it you want from me?"

As they clearly belonged to Hamas Security, I did show them my passport, with the same gesture asking Taher's children to hide my laptop.

The bearded man asked me, "Who is the *muhrem* accompanying you?"

A *muhrem* is a father, husband or brother who must be responsible for a woman.

"What *muhrem*? I'm twenty-eight-years old and have no need of a *muhrem*. This is my father's number. Call him and tell him where his daughter is. What's all this about, have you gone insane?"

He started to thunder, "You... you..."

"What do you mean: you? We've done nothing wrong."

May's brother had disappeared. They'd arrested him without anyone noticing. Zeina, Taher's wife, intervened. "If she'd been wearing a niqab you'd have left her alone. She could have shut herself away with a man if she'd wanted to. You've followed her simply because she's going bareheaded. That's what her crime is."

We continued to argue with them like that. Then Taher called a mutual friend who had become a government spokesman.

"Listen, there are some men here who want to arrest Asmaa."

"But what's gotten into them?"

He asked to speak to them, which he did, but that had no effect. This was a hint at the shift that was taking place: in a matter such as this, the Hamas government spokesman had less power than a little 'morality policeman'. I recalled the arrogance of the stretcher-bearer. He didn't care who I was or what role I was playing at the time; for him I was just another indecent woman who needed to be veiled. Another journalist friend close to Hamas intervened with the bearded man on the beach but to no greater effect. He was absolutely determined to take me away, and I absolutely refused to follow him.

My friend May arrived, beside herself. "Some armed men have surrounded the cafeteria. They threatened us with their machine pistols, they took the boys away, it's crazy!"

The officer gave me my passport back, apparently he'd decided to leave without me. "Just you be careful," he said, "we'll be keeping an eye on you."

"As for me, I won't forget what you did."

We went home and told our parents everything. Then we decided to sleep, but in vain. The young people were released at two in the morning after having been thoroughly beaten and forced to sign an 'undertaking', according to which they would never contravene the Islamic laws again. It was the first time this practice had been heard of in Gaza. I had been naive. In 2007, Hamas had attained power by violence; in 2008, Israel had started a war that had broken us but reinforced Hamas, the party finding itself sole master of a destroyed and sealed-off territory. In other words, we were in their hands. The aim of Hamas wasn't to administer the captive society it controlled but to realize its dream of Islamizing it at top speed, and that was what it was doing.

The very next day we went with May, her brothers and relations, to see the human rights organizations. In the meantime we had heard what the police had asked the young people who had been taken in. Of one: "Have you slept with Asmaa?" Of another, May's brother, "You went with Asmaa and left one of your friends behind you with your sister. How do you know he didn't take advantage of that to sleep with her behind your back?"

All these cretins could talk about was sex, it was a real obsession. They thought no other relationship was possible between people. And I suddenly discovered that this was not an isolated event. A large number of young people had, like us, been subjected to degrading treatment but hadn't dared to complain. The moral interdict had been internalized and spread in silence!

In the interview I gave on the *Al Arabiya* website, I explained how the Hamas government was trying to use women's bodies and relationships between boys and girls to make people feel ashamed: "This government wants to make people believe that it's there to defend us, to preserve our women and girls, but in reality they're not protecting us at all, they're attacking our private life. That is the truth about what they're doing and it has to be said."

At the time, I had no idea of the impact this interview was going to have—more that three hundred comments on the *Al Arabiya* site in the following hours. It echoed through the whole of Gaza to the point where people recognized me and called out to me in the street. Some congratulated me for my courage, others were indignant and reproached me for having spoken out. Girls who claimed to be liberal said, "You've aroused negative reactions, doesn't that frighten you?" But what were they talking about? These girls allowed themselves all sorts of things abroad and played at being good little conservatives once they were back in Gaza. It's strange. They wanted me to let myself be oppressed while remaining silent for fear of scandal.

Now the scandal was there, but not the one the girls imagined. The head of the police picked up his phone to ask me if everything I had described was true.

"You think I was lying?" I replied.

"If it is true, then we will offer you our apologies."

"You'd do better to go and see your policemen and investigate."

"That's what I'm going to do and I'll get back to you."

Naturally I never heard from him again. Eventually Taher started to get scared. "Asmaa," he said, "don't mention me in connection with this business again."

This was the man who'd let me into his beach hut and defended me together with his wife, my journalist colleague—I couldn't believe my ears.

"Listen," I replied, "since you're asking, I won't mention your name again. But no one's going to stop me talking about what happened. It's my right and I'm not afraid of anyone."

At first my father encouraged me: "You've done nothing wrong, go ahead." But as the counter-pressures increased, he said, "Why do you have to talk so much? Keep your head down."

The more I refused to step back, the more the press wanted to interview me. The foreign media had taken up the affair. As well as creating a plainclothes morality police force, the government had imposed the hijab on girls at school, on lawyers, on civil servants... Drawing courage, people who had remained silent until then started to talk about their own experiences of repression. We began to get together to organize the struggle against the obligation to wear the hijab, we set up citizens' action groups that brought together lawyers, left-wingers, democrats... Every day I was declaring that Hamas was interfering in people's private life, just as the Somali tribunals or the Islamic government in the Sudan did. At the same time, a young Sudanese journalist called Lubna Hussein had been sentenced to be whipped for wearing tight trousers. An international campaign had been organized to support her. Journalists started writing articles linking us: 'Lubna and Asmaa' became the two faces of the resistance to the governments that were using Islam to control society.

People thought I had a score to settle with Hamas and with them alone. However often I told them that wasn't the case, that it was a matter of principle, they only half believed me.

One day a man on crutches arrived in my office at *Al Ayyam*. "I've heard that you're a woman who isn't afraid," he said.

"Yes?"

"I have a big story I'd like to tell you."

"I'm listening."

"I am the man who, during the second Intifada, managed to raise a Palestinian flag over Netzarim, the Israeli military base in Gaza. The photo went around the world, you must have seen it. I took a bullet in the leg during the operation. If it wasn't properly treated my leg could develop gangrene, which is what happened. There was a risk of my losing it so I got them to transfer me from Gaza to the West Bank. On the way to the hospital I was captured by military intelligence agents of the Palestine Authority, who kept me in prison for a month. After that they sent me back to Gaza with a leg that was completely ruined. Are you prepared to tell my story?"

"If I can verify it, yes."

He revealed everything to me, how the military intelligence service had treated him, what he'd seen, the people who'd been tortured, the prisoners kept without water, the old men whose only crime was to be members of Hamas. He himself was suspected of having been sent by the Islamist movement to the West Bank on a spying mission. "I was beaten and humiliated, and no one wanted to listen to my story. So I taught my son to hate them and to kill them when he grows up..."

At the time when, day after day, I was reporting the

abuses committed by Hamas, this man had come to tell me of similar acts committed by Fatah. For my research on the matter I contacted an officer of the Fatah security service who said, "What this guy's telling you isn't true, we did nothing to him."

"So you admit you did have him."

"Yes."

"Okay, that's good enough for me. How long did you keep him?"

"About a month."

During our conversation the officer told me the man had tried to commit suicide with a razor blade. I sent my article to *Al Ayyam*. That paper isn't dependent on Fatah, but since the separation of Gaza and the West Bank any journal has more or less taken a certain stance for or against. The secretary of the Journalists' Association and director of *Al Ayyam* called me.

"Are you out of your mind, sending us an article like that? What's gotten into you? I haven't even shown it to the editor. Do you want them to dismiss you?"

I took back my article and sent it to *Amine*, a website that published brave testimonies against both Fatah and Hamas. It was the beginning of the blogs. For the first time ever, Hamas took over my article and put it in their journal *Palestine*. That was in 2009. *Al Ayyam* started rejecting my articles, and personal problems with the director made the situation even worse. I asked for leave without pay, which was refused, so I decided to hand in my resignation.

That left me with nothing, no money, no work, no means. My only remaining source of income was *Skeyes*, the foundation for the freedom of the press, but they only paid me by the article and I couldn't invent attacks on our freedom simply in order to have something to write. I was forced to borrow money from my friends, which I still haven't finished paying back. All that was left to me was political campaigning and my blog, where I placed everything I should have been sending to *Al Ayyam*. But they are not the kind of thing people expect from a blog, so I started to write on that shifting frontier between what I knew, what I thought and what I was living through—in a way, I was reconnecting with literature.

23

Riding a Bicycle

I WAS DRIVING TOWARD RAFAH with three friends from abroad when we heard that the Ministry of the Interior had decided to forbid women to ride bicycles and motorbikes. The minister had apparently been disturbed by the sight of a woman pedaling—he saw in it a "distinctly sexual connotation." We had a good laugh at that. The Islamists, who claim they detest Freud, are those who most prove him right. They see sex everywhere—in a pair of lips sucking on the mouthpiece of a hookah as much as in the movement of a female butt on the saddle of a bicycle. The funniest thing was that my companions, an Italian couple and an American woman, had intended to cycle back from Rafah to Gaza, their bikes being attached to the roof of the car. Another female friend who was to be on the trip had let them down at the last minute so that there was one extra bicycle.

"How about you cycling back with us?" they asked me.

I said no. We drove on in silence but the idea was going around and around in my head. The distance between the two towns was some forty kilometers. That's a long way, and it was right in the middle of Ramadan and very hot; I just wouldn't be able to manage it. When I was six, my father had brought a bike back from the Emirates for me; he taught me how to ride it before taking off the two stabilizers. Later, when I was in the Gulf myself, a neighbor regularly used to let me borrow his bike, but that was a long time ago. I was afraid I might fall off and injure myself, that was surely it. There was, of course, another reason that I didn't admit to: I had no desire to get into trouble with Hamas again. Why did it always have to be me? Why did I always have to end up in the limelight, 'in the cannon's mouth' as we say in Arabic. I had the right to be left in peace. But when my friends asked me again, I replied without hesitation, "Okay, I'll come with you."

Our departure point was the border between Egypt and Gaza. My friends tried to lower the saddle of my bicycle because it was too high for me, but without success. Neighbors of ours in Rafah came with adjustable wrenches and worked on it as if we were going on a great expedition. I mounted the bike, made some progress, wobbled a bit, put my foot on the ground and said I'd changed my mind. My friends were insistent, I couldn't give up the idea I had hardly started. I tried again and just kept going, leaving my friends to catch up with me.

We met up on the road. Now and then we passed policemen. Perhaps they thought we were a group of foreign cyclists who needed to be protected. They surrounded us for a moment, then let us go on our way. Some people laughed, others gave us a friendly wave. There were also some who insulted us—in their eyes we were doubtless doing something scandalous. Two bearded men on motorcycles suddenly started pursuing us. When they overtook, one of them spat at me and the other hit my American friend hard on the back. We kept going.

Other bikers followed us—two young men with unpleasant expressions overtook us, waited for us to catch up, then repeated the ploy. I realized we weren't going to get rid of them. I saw a police van, stopped and reported them quite openly. Despite the ban on women cycling, the police helped us willingly. They bawled the young men out, held them back and gestured to us to go on. When they said goodbye, I waved in reply and fell off. The policemen burst out laughing.

I fell off three more times. The ride was as long as expected, I was literally exhausted, drained from the heat, and I almost fainted twice because I hadn't eaten since the previous evening. My friends regularly splashed water over my face. We stopped now and then to take a breather, repair our bikes or blow up a tire. People would ask us, "Are you fasting? Are you Muslims?" They would ask the most hateful question, "Christians or Muslims?" In the past people didn't dare ask that kind of question, it was shameful. But your religion has become more important than your country. No one asks, "Are you Palestinian like me?" any longer but, "Are you a Muslim like me?" It's this confessionalism that is the disaster.

We eventually arrived in Gaza, not without some difficulty. Our bicycle adventure, which I recounted in my blog, provoked the same fuss as the beach episode: there were those who congratulated me, those who held it against me and let me know it; there were all sorts of impassioned reactions as if the trip from From Rafah to Gaza, through which I'd lost several kilos, was a question of supreme importance. I kept nothing back, I said that no one had opposed us, we hadn't been held up at a single checkpoint. That perhaps meant that the minister's decisions were taken by a self-satisfied kind of guy, sitting in his armchair surrounded by the four women he'd married legitimately: "And what would you say if I were to ban cycling? Or if I made the hookah unlawful?" I imagined the scene. It is true that the Minister of the Interior did indeed have four wives...

Despite everything, there have never been many women cycling on the roads of Gaza. The document forbidding this activity was not a law but a simple 'decision' of the Minister. No one voted for it anymore than they had for the decisions recommending that women should cover their heads or not wear short-sleeved blouses. Women submitted to them so as to do the same as everyone else, to avoid standing out, to be 'decent'. Islamization makes its appearance as a general mood. War had made the Islamist regime more persnickety— in fact, it makes all regimes more persnickety—and the people followed suit. For example, do you know why a woman carries her marriage contract in her handbag? Because she might be required to show it if she should happen to be caught walking hand-in-hand with her husband... People seem quite happy to obey, to allow themselves to be controlled. They sometimes even anticipate the demand, overdo it when no one is asking anything of them. One day the headmistress insisted my sisters cover their heads and punished them when they refused to, making them stand there in the blazing sun.

I went to see her to protest. She replied, "I wanted to do a good deed before God."

"But... are you a headmistress or a missionary?"

Then I notified the Ministry of Education and an official went to the school with me. In my presence he signed a letter formally requiring the headmistress to no longer involve herself in making her pupils wear veils and she obeyed. But in the meantime my sisters had made their own decision to wear the hijab. They were afraid to tell me, so my mother did. I told her, "But they're free to do so." I said that, then I went and locked myself in my room, where I cried the whole night. On the pretext of exercising a 'free choice' they had yielded to the pressure.

24

The Tunisian Torch

MY FRIENDS AND I told each other that the Islamization of society was proceeding naturally, without a
sound, as if everyone was fast asleep. "Isha!" ("Wake up!")
was the name we chose for our movement. It was around the
middle of 2010, well before the outbreak of the Arab Spring.
There were about fifteen of us, young people of both sexes
who had no awareness of being precursors. Our first press
release was a protest against the closure of the Sharek Youth
Forum, an extremely active institution financed by the
European Union and the United Nations, which organized
summer camps together with UNRWA and all kinds of
secular activities, bringing together moderate Islamists,
liberals and ordinary people.

Hamas accused it of promoting the mixing of girls and
boys and encouraging "morally reprehensible behavior." As
soon as they became aware of our press release they
demanded that the director of Sharek obtain a formal re-
traction from us, failing which they would not allow the
institution to reopen. We naturally refused to yield to this
blackmail and called for a demonstration in support of
Sharek—which has remained closed to this day.

Our second press release was to protest against the
decision to impose the wearing of the hijab in schools and to
reaffirm that secular identity was one of the component

parts of Gaza society and had to be respected. The Hamas government was furious—they realized that from now on we were going to keep a close eye on them. Their Security started to summon the members of Isha! one by one and harass them. But we were not alone. In order to create a minimum balance of power we maintained close relationships with the foreign media. As a sign of the times another movement was started, the Association of Young Secularists with which we joined forces to organize a number of seminars. The first opposition movement to the Islamic government in Gaza was emerging.

At that point, I was invited to Denmark: I had won a competition organized by Freedom House, an American NGO that honored articles dealing with various aspects of freedom. In Copenhagen I met the editor who had authorized the publication of the caricatures of the Prophet, which had provoked the huge scandal everyone has heard about. I didn't approve of the publication of those caricatures but I was in favor of the freedom of thought and expression. That is what I wrote in my blog, adding that this freedom was more important than religious freedom—because if the former is assured then the latter will inevitably be as well, while if the freedom of religion takes precedence, it will crush all others.

Back in Gaza I found on my blog a letter addressed to me personally: death threats signed "Jaysh al Islam" ("Army of Islam"). Was it because I'd campaigned against the closure of Sharek? Because I'd talked about the Danish journalist when I expressed my opinion of the caricatures of the Prophet? I had no idea. Over the next few days the threats on my blog were repeated, then came the time when the threats were on my telephone. So I decided to report this to the police. As usual they refused to record my complaint. Frightened, I went to Egypt to wait until things calmed down.

So I was in Egypt, sitting at a table in a café with a friend, when the photos of a Tunisian street vendor by the name of Mohamed Bouazizi appeared in the newspapers: he had tried to burn himself to death in southern Tunisia. It was December 17, 2010. At that point no one could imagine that less than two months later the incident was going to set off the Arab Spring, the fall of the Tunisian president, Ben Ali, and that of the Egyptian president, Hosni Mubarak. In Cairo, I was hosting a seminar attended by many Tunisians who helped me to follow the course of the uprising. Demonstrations demanding that Ben Ali should step down were increasing day by day in Tunisia. The President made some concessions, but too little too late. Eventually he appeared on TV to make the famous speech in which he said, "I have understood you." The Tunisians around me burst out laughing. "It's over. That speech is the speech of the end." I remained skeptical until my sister phoned from Tunis, saying, "Ben Ali has fled!"

That day I was with the same friend in the same Cairo café. My sister continued, "He got on the plane, but the pilot refused to take off so as not to aid him in his flight. Finally he managed to change plane and escape." I switched off my phone and announced the news to the whole café but no one believed me. It was too soon; less than a month had passed since Bouazizi had tried to set himself on fire and less than ten days since his death. The news was very quickly officially confirmed. I then called my Tunisian friends and we all started to laugh on the phone. We were so happy!

Raring to go, I returned to Gaza to take part in the demonstration we had organized with the Young Secularists to protest against the closure of Sharek. The atmosphere was particularly tense, the police there in huge numbers and the clashes started even before our sparse procession headed out. The police started by arresting eighteen people, all boys (including my brother Mustafa) apart from one woman who, unfortunately for them, was the correspondent of *Al Jazeera International*. During the night the authorities realized what a blunder they'd made and started to release some of the young people and the journalist. The only ones left behind bars were the two young organizers of the movement... and my brother Mustafa. Why him? Some officers had come into their cell where they were all being held and asked, "Who is the brother of Asmaa al-Ghoul?" and he'd put up his hand.

The following day he was the only one left in prison, the two others had been released. His lawyer was told, "If Asmaa gives herself up, he will be released."

"But why should she give herself up?"

"Because she hit a policeman."

I was beside myself at that. "I never hit a policeman, I just pushed his arm away when he was trying to film me." During this time Mustafa was slapped, beaten, and the police tried to humiliate him by all possible means. In particular they tried to force him to pray and when he refused, they accused him of an "offense against religion," a crime punishable by six months in prison. Interior Security finally handed him over to the police, where I was able to visit him. I found him sitting down, tousled, a blank look on his face, dazed from the blows and humiliations. The State Attorney, who had summoned him, had asked, "How can you allow your sister to go the demonstrations with young people? You are lax in religion because you allow her to behave badly." I posted that mind-boggling declaration on my blog and called for solidarity with my brother. The slogan "Free Mustafa al-Ghoul!" spread and photos of Mustafa appeared in the streets. A Hamas member of parliament, who was a bit smarter than the rest, realized Security was trying to get at me through my brother and that the affair was counter-productive for the government. He went to see the Attorney who a little later ordered Mustafa to be released. In the end they got nothing out of it.

This affair had barely been sorted out when I heard that another of my brothers, Abdullah, had just been arrested in Egypt, accused of having photographed a military zone while taking pictures with his girlfriend in the Suez Canal area. I rushed to Cairo and, with the help of various people, managed to get him released. As we were about to head off together for the border, I noticed that there were lots of police and officers of the Egyptian intelligence services out in the streets and that they looked particularly agitated. It was January 24, 2011. The next day, back in Gaza, I opened my Facebook page to discover that the revolution had broken out in Egypt on that very day. I tore my hair—why hadn't I stayed? What a lousy journalist I was. An American colleague and I dashed to the border to go back to Egypt. Too late! The door had closed. My colleague immediately went to Israel and was able to get to Cairo via Tel Aviv, but that was forbidden to me. For some unknown reason, since 2001 I had been on a blacklist that made it impossible for me to enter Israel. At least the Hamas, Fatah and Israeli authorities all agreed about me, thank God!

25

General Salwa

EVERYTHING SUDDENLY started to accelerate. The Tunisian people had thrown out their president seventeen days ago, the Egyptian people had been camping in Tahrir Square for six days, demanding with loud cries the fall of Mubarak—we thought we were dreaming! With a simple slogan: "The people want the fall of the regime," and a clear command: "Clear off!" the population of those two countries had spewed out decades of oppression and caught dictatorships that had believed themselves to be eternal off their guard. Similar signs were making themselves felt in Bahrain, in Syria, in Libya, in Yemen... We were quivering. Those young people in Tunis or Cairo, who are taking all the risks because they have a foretaste of freedom on their lips, are our doubles, they are ourselves. Has the crazy longing for a world that is free, dignified and democratic finally reached our shores? On this morning of January 31, 2011, the day of Gaza's solidarity with the Egyptian revolution, I can still believe it.

At the moment when I arrive at the Square of the Unknown Soldier I hear my name crackling on the walkie-talkies of the Hamas plainclothes police: "Asmaa al-Ghoul has arrived!" I look around for the Palestinian blogger from whom the appeal for a demonstration came. I'm told that an important meeting has prevented her from coming—later she admits that she gave way to the threats telling her not to attend the demo. In support of the glorious revolution on the banks of the Nile there are, all in all... eight of us, three men and five women, two of whom are veiled. The Hamas intelligence agents come slowly toward us. I recognize their faces, the white car and the unmarked van that I had noticed when my brother was arrested. They come and order us to disperse. We refuse. The three men are immediately taken away. Then it's our turn. A cop grabs one of the veiled women and tries to drag her away. I shout, "Aren't you a Muslim? Aren't you forbidden to touch women? Leave her alone." At that very moment two policewomen turn up behind me. "Where's Asmaa al-Ghoul? We're looking for her." In order to escape them I run over to a man belonging to a human rights organization. "They want to arrest me," I tell him, but he looks the other way. A coward. The policewomen get me; soon all five of us are in the van. They confiscate our belong-ings, our papers, our cell phones, etc. One policeman says to me with a carnivorous smile, "Asmaa al-Ghoul, at last! *Ahlan wa sahlan!* Welcome," and they all start to insult us, they don't stop during the whole journey. "We're going to make you shut your mouths," "You won't be able to say another word," and the whole array of disgusting insults. Calmly I ask, "Is Officer Badawi with you?"

A bespectacled guy replies, "Badawi? What d'you want from him?'

"Nothing. I just want to know if he's here."

At the police station we're separated, the men are taken to the male block, we to the female one. It's an area where the Hamas female officers operate. One of the women who has been taken into custody is a correspondent for a human rights NGO—she was there to report, not to demonstrate. However, she can't stop crying. I tell her in English that we shouldn't show any signs of weakness and that she should control herself. One of the policewomen shouts, "Don't speak English." Immediately we all turn to English. I tell the girls, "No one must sign a declaration." A little later one of the female officers comes to see me.

"Are you the one in charge of this group?"

"No, I'm not in charge of anyone."

"So why do the others refuse to sign their declaration?"

"They're free to do so or not. I've told them nothing."

She senses that's not true, but she can't prove anything. She asks the group, "Which mosque is closest to your home?" because, unfortunately, the mosques are the antennas of Hamas Intelligence in Gaza. In each one the imam writes a report on the district he is in charge of. The intelligence services will ask the imam to tell them everything he knows about you, and he will reply from a perspective in which he, of course, represents good and those he keeps under sur- veillance, evil. When we hear the question, we start laughing and the policewomen get annoyed. "Don't laugh!" The veiled militants ask for carpets because it's sunset prayer time.

The policewomen mock them as if they owned the religion, "Why do you demonstrate with these women who don't even wear the hijab?" they ask, pointing at us.

"Because when they see people like you representing Islam they start hating all the religions God created. But when they see us, there's still a chance."

The policewomen don't know what to say, it's true that they're not the brightest. Completely veiled apart from their eyes, they're told never to call each other by their names so they won't be recognized, but they keep forgetting that all the time. I spot one who's called Salwa, she's trying to intimidate the women, "We're going to lock you up in prison with women of ill repute. Don't think you're going to be treated as militants."

Then my turn comes. Salwa takes me into a neighboring

room, makes me stand by the wall and starts hitting me and pulling my hair. I tell her, "I've just had an operation, don't hit me on the scar," at which she starts hitting me precisely on that spot.

The door opens and another policewoman comes in, and during that time one of my comrades sees me being hit. Salwa bawls out her colleague for opening the door then she turns back to me, heaping reproaches on me for criticizing the government and campaigning for an Arab Spring in Gaza. At least she's understood that. She starts hitting me again, on my face and my neck, screaming, "You're not a Muslim!"

"Why? Are you one? You pull my hair, you squeeze my face under your arm and you think you're a Muslim. You think you're more Muslim than I am because my hair is uncovered?"

"Yes, I'm a Muslim."

"No, you're not. You're hitting me unjustly."

"No. I'm correcting you, I'm reforming you, that's part of Islam."

I continue to answer her back with a strength I didn't know I had in me. I tell her, "You'll see. I'm going to describe exactly what you do, and then the whole world will know..."

She goes out to see her colleagues. I hear her say, "She says that she's going to tell everything, that she's going to drag me through the mud."

Then several of them come back and order me to speak— they seriously believe I'm going to change my mind because I've been hit a few times. Salwa mutters to one of her colleagues, "She'd prepared herself." What can she mean by that? How can you prepare yourself for being beaten without opening your mouth?

Given the policewomen's poor results, a certain Yussef arrives, a nasty piece of work. He takes a pencil, puts it close to my face and threatens to stick it into my cheek, shouting, "Speak! Speak!" I know what he wants me to say: who the women with me are, who is behind us, do we have any connections with Ramallah? That's because the most serious accusation is to be in league with their rivals Fatah. Once Yussef has left empty-handed, I say to Salwa, "You want me to speak?"

"Yes."

"Well start by saying you're sorry."

"I'm sorry," she says immediately.

We could have been in a Russian play. I go on, "Good. Okay then, now you can ask me some questions."

"Did you organize the demo?"

"No."

"Who organized it?"

"I don't know."

"How did you get to know the other girls?"

"On Facebook."

She goes crazy. "But you're not telling me anything at all!"

She goes out. I hear her say to her colleagues. "I'd like us to finish now because I've been invited to a wedding." She talks about her father, who refuses to eat his meals as long as she's not in the house. She says, "Papa always says, 'Where's the General?' when he's talking about me."

A slightly more polite police officer comes in. "Your father and your son have come to see you. Your son has brought some things, but your father argued with the officer who eventually sent him out because he was... disrespectful."

He takes me to the officer in question, a certain Tayeb.

"I want you to sign your declaration."

"I will not sign any declaration."

"Your father has come, but he supports you. That is why we refused to hand you over to him."

"That's not important, I can go by myself. And I will not sign anything."

"All the girls have signed."

"That's because you told them Asmaa had signed. You told every one the others had signed, didn't you?

"No."

"You did. Those are you methods."

In fact, negotiations had taken place involving the lawyers, journalists and prominent figures who had tried to obtain our release from outside by pressing for the girls' declarations to be modified to make them more favorable. In fact the most negative parts of the depositions had been deleted, which was a victory in itself. But I continue to refuse to sign even the modified version.

He says, "When you arrived you asked about an officer called Badawi. Why?"

"When our friends were imprisoned during the last demonstration, Badawi went to meet their parents and said to them, 'Asmaa has slept with the leader of the youth movement, and also with so-and-so and so-and-so.' According-ing to the religion that defamation constitutes a *kazef mohsanat,* the sin of publicly defaming a woman's honor which brings a severe punishment. And that Badawi raised his arm to threaten my brother in prison. There is now a personal *tar*[4] between me and him, and I am going to lodge a complaint against him with the Prime Minister."

To my great surprise the bespectacled little man who was sitting in the car with us jumps up out of his seat and reveals himself: he is Badawi. "No, no, I said nothing like that!"

"You certainly said it. I have witnesses who will testify against you. And you will have me breathing down your neck

4 *tar*: vendetta

until justice is done and my name is cleared."

The officer was embarrassed. He didn't expect a so-called 'liberal' woman to be concerned about her honor to the point of accusing by name a policeman of having besmirched it. Badawi doubtless believed he had the right to insult me with impunity—I go around bareheaded, which means I'm 'dirty' and lacking dignity.

He says to me, "You don't want to sign your declaration, okay. But you have to sign some paper or other for me."

So I tear a page out of my notebook and cut out a tiny piece that has just enough room for my signature and no more. I scribble my name on it, get up and leave without a word. It's eight or nine in the evening, and there's a cold wind. A policeman on a motorbike asks me, "Would you like me to accompany you?"

I recognize him; he's the one who told me my father and brother had come to see me in prison. I still say no thanks, however. He says, "My mother has made a nice *maftoul* for dinner." He's nice. He goes off, and I make my way home. How I loved that walk! The fresh air gradually soothed the fire I could feel inside me.

Back home I wrote a post that became famous: "General Salwa." In it I wrote how I set out to show my solidarity with the Egyptian revolution and ended up with my head stuck under a policewoman's arm. I reported all the details of our arrest, making the 'General' look ridiculous, giving her a reputation she would doubtless have preferred not to have. A few days later the Director of the Women's Police came to the office to apologize to me. "I'm sorry. I've read what you wrote on your blog. These policewomen are used to interrogating suspects regarding common rather than political rights." That was the start of a long discussion. She was extremely courteous but was accompanied by a pretty vindictive woman, who said, "I read your blog regularly and

I am not at all in agreement with you. What you write is anti-Islam."

I replied, "On the contrary, I am restoring the image of Islam that you have damaged. If you imagine that you of Hamas represent Islam then that is a real catastrophe."

When they heard how the 'General' had hit me, some of my friends said they were prepared to go and beat her up, but I was happy that the Director of Women's Police had come to apologize. That didn't stop me still having nightmares for nights on end. In the meantime this traumatic experience had made me widely known, it supported my nomination for the prize of the Deutsche Villa. But I remain ambivalent about these prizes: I keep wondering whether I really deserve them. However that may be, the affair put me on the list of the "most influential personalities in the Arab world" published in the Spanish version of the journal *Foreign Policy*. I can't say it's a great consolation, but it does help.

26

Men in Pajamas

THE KICK-OFF FOR the Palestinian Spring is to be given by a large demonstration on March 15, 2011, both on the West Bank and in Gaza. That is what we have decided. We can't join the other Arab nations in demanding "the fall of the regime" because we have two regimes—and we won't get anywhere as long as the split between Fatah and Hamas persists. For us it will rather be "The people want national unity," and that is the slogan we have adopted. A movement that has taken the name of "The Youth of March 15" has also called for the demonstration. The boldest is GYBO (Gaza Youth Breaks Out), a collective of young militants which has made a name for itself with an inflammatory manifesto: "To hell with Hamas. To hell with Israel. To hell with Fatah... We, the young people of Gaza, are fed up with all this. We're like fleas stuck between two fingernails, we're living out a nightmare within another nightmare." There were just three of them at the start but they quickly attracted incredible support. The Association of Young Secularists and Isha! were also part of the collective calling for the demonstration.

The Hamas agencies were not slow to react. They rounded up and interrogated all the militants they managed to identify. At first they didn't bother me but summoned my father to get him to put pressure on me and prevent me from writing.

"How could I tell my daughter of twenty-nine to stop writing?" he replied.

"You're responsible for her."

"That is your opinion. As for me, I stopped being responsible for her a long time ago. You can continue to give orders to your children and govern them until they die, but for me, that's not the way things are. I leave them free."

He came home somewhat upset by the lack of respect with which he'd been treated. He told me, "The message they have for you is: 'Don't write anything anymore.' Well, what I'm saying to you is, 'Go on writing. Don't fear anyone.'" He smiled before adding, "I had no idea how afraid of you they are."

In reality, what they were afraid of was the movement as a whole, and quite rightly so: the young people throughout the Arab world were in turmoil and the question of Palestinian unity that we had chosen seemed to be a key issue. The Hamas leaders guessed that they weren't going to be confronted with the usual minor demonstration but with a mass movement.

It's the morning of March 15 and I'm heading for Seraglio Square, the setting-off point for the demo. I'm met by a forest of Hamas flags. There's a considerable crowd, but I can't recognize anyone. The Islamist movement in power has fabricated a so-called "Youth Association" that has trumpeted its support for March 15. Making colossal efforts, they have called for the gathering by putting up posters everywhere. Fatah has done the same on the West Bank: mobilized the population in the same way, outflanking our comrades over there. The fraternal enemies were pretending to join the movement. They even claimed to have originated the idea, swearing, hand on heart, that they were against the divisions and for the unity of Palestine.

Sick at heart, my friends and I leave and set off at a brisk pace for another large square in the town, that of the Unknown Soldier. Young members of Hamas and the Islamic Jihad get in our way. They stick to us. On the way we pass several *zannane*, Hamas's little spies, kids who try to attack and hit us. We give them a few blows in return and continue on our way. The Square of the Unknown Soldier is also covered in Hamas flags, the leaders have already started to speak, relayed by a powerful PA system. They're stealing our day and the most important squares in the town.

I think about a place that won't have occurred to them: Al Khatib Square, a green space four times the size of the place where we are at the moment. I shout, "Everyone to Al Khatib." The Jihad and Fatah militants send me messages saying that's not a good idea, but I don't take orders from anyone. There's not a soul on Al Khatib Square. I send a torrent of messages on my cell phone: "There's already ten thousand of us! Come and join us." It's a brazen lie, but I have no choice. All our friends who were getting nowhere at the Seraglio or at the Unknown Soldier converge on the square. One hour later, we're not far from being thirty thousand—at least that's what I say in my text messages. The institutions, the trade unions, the journalists, everyone joins the movement. We're euphoric. We don't have a PA system, we have to improvise. We strike up patriotic songs and shout slogans, that's all we can do. Security arrive and start filming us; we can see from their faces how furious they are: we've managed to make them look ridiculous. Someone comes to tell me our people are terribly thirsty, Hamas having given instructions that water is not to be delivered to us. We manage to get two water tanks towed to the square, and all we just have to do is help ourselves from the taps—it's so hot!

Now people are flooding in from all directions, there are more and more of us. Some have brought tents and we decide to sleep there, like our comrades in Cairo's Tahir Square.

Our morale is as high as can be, the Hamas Prime Minister himself has the audacity to make a speech saying that he supports us... Our March 15 is a great success. At 5:30 p.m., rumors start to go around that the government is preparing to launch an attack on us but we just shrug our shoulders and retain our optimism. I come across a friend in the crowd, Samah el Sheikh, who is an actor and writer. Pregnant, she's come to the demonstration with her poet husband and their daughter. Over by the mosque I suddenly notice men in pajamas armed with batons who are rushing at the crowd with loud cries. I guess that they're the regime's henchmen coming from prayers. They're wearing pajamas to make people think they're simple civilians who've come as local inhabitants. Samah's husband takes their daughter by the hand and hurries away with her. I start running as well, I see people beaten up, girls hit, women dragged along the ground and subjected to copious insults: "Whores! Women of ill repute! Your children are prostitutes like you!"

I manage to get out of the square and hurry toward a main road where the traffic is heavier, hoping to escape that way. But a man in pajamas armed with a thin iron rod starts chasing me. He catches up with me on the edge of a sidewalk and starts to beat me. "You're Asmaa al-Ghoul, aren't you? It is you?" I shout, "That's enough! Leave me alone!" Rather than coming to help me, the people keep as far away as possible—while a few minutes ago on the square they were all gathering around me. Eventually I manage to escape from my attacker and run into a dark, narrow street. At that moment I hear the voice of my friend Samah behind me: a dozen Security men have cornered her and are beating her up. I have to admit that I hesitate for a second, then retrace my steps. Samah is much bigger than me, I have no idea how I manage to push the men out of the way and put my arms around her, covering her completely. When she tells the story today she says, "Asmaa managed to put me inside her." And the blows start to rain down on my head and shoulders while the men in pajamas shout our names, hers and mine. No one comes to help us, except a person you'd never expect to see, a man called Ghassan, neither a militant, nor a writer, nor a poet... a simple bookkeeper. He'd been taking part in the gathering, and when he saw us being beaten he just ran over to help us. Suddenly Samah said to me, "I can feel something in my back." A stab with a knife.

Someone I know arrives: Yussef, the man who threatened to make a hole in my cheek with a pencil. He shouts at me, "Are you going to call me Abul Zalaam (the father of oppression) again?" He's been doing some reading—that's what I called him in my blog. He has us arrested, Sameh and me. As for the unfortunate Ghassan, he orders him to be taken in as well.

At the Security prison I see a line of cameras and tape recorders the plainclothes officers have smashed, cameras that have been seized, even the goods confiscated from the poor vendors of fruit juice. Above all, I witness the comings and goings of the men in pajamas who come for a rest. They behave as if they belong there, which they do. A warder asks me to come and see Sameh, who's sitting in a neighboring room. She's in a bad way. The knife penetrated the fat and muscles; no sensitive organ seems to have been affected but the wound doesn't look good. Another officer arrives who makes me stand up against the wall and slowly comes up to me.

"Aren't you afraid?"

"No."

"We hit women as well, you know."

"I don't believe you."

Sameh starts shouting, "Leave her alone!"

He insults both of us and comes back to me. "Where's

your son Nasser? Wasn't he with your mother in the garden yesterday? And where is he today?"

Suddenly we're both very much afraid, we don't say a single word. We can see that the man is satisfied. "You can write what you like about me."

That's all they're worried about: what I can write. I remain silent. He goes on, "If I see a single sentence, a single letter you've written about me, you'd better look out."

An officer comes with some cotton and some alcohol and asks me to clean Sameh's wound. I refuse, saying, "It's a deep wound, my friend could fall unconscious. You've got to call an ambulance to take her to the hospital."

They don't know what to do, they hesitate for a good hour before picking up the phone. And when they do, they register Sameh under a made-up name. I ask to go to the washroom, and the officer orders his men to accompany me. "And don't let her in the toilet with the eucalyptus outside the window," he shouts. He clearly follows what I write. The last time I was imprisoned I noticed that tree outside the window. Parts of the way I took to school when I was little, sick with fear of the Israelis, were planted with eucalyptus. For some inexplicable reason the scent of that tree gave me a feeling of safety, so that I had been reassured by the prison eucalyptus, and I'd recounted that in my piece about 'General Salwa'.

When I come out of the toilet, I'm taken to a room and a completely veiled woman comes in behind me. I say, "We're alone, there are no men with us, why do you keep your niqab on?"

Without a word she takes it off and I say, "Allah! You look like my mother."

It's true! We start to talk. It becomes almost friendly. She asks, "Why did you demonstrate?"

"But that's obvious. Everyone knew about it the day

before. Please ask me questions you don't know the reply to."

An officer bursts into the room, interrupting us. A message from my friend Fathi arrived on my cell phone a moment ago: "The meeting is fixed for eight o'clock at the Institute."

The officer says, "We went to the Institute, there was no one there. Call your friend back and ask what the new place for the meeting is so we can go there."

He really thinks I'm going to spy for him. I say, "Okay, Call back the number."

He does so and puts his ear next to mine. I feel he gets a bit too close.

"Hello?"

"Fathi?"

"Asmaa, where are you? We've been looking for you everywhere."

"I'm at Security, they've beaten me."

The officer brutally cuts off the call, picks up an iron chair and holds it over my head. I protect myself and cry, "I'm sorry, I'm sorry, I couldn't do anything else."

And it's true, no one knew I'd been taken in by Security and I've managed to sound the alarm.

The veiled woman reproaches me bitterly. "I was good to you because you played at being nice. It's my fault. I allowed you to become familiar with me."

Officer Tayeb comes back into the room, his tone is slightly more courteous, "You have to state that our men didn't attack you, you fought amongst yourselves."

He demands that because outside, though I don't know this yet, things are starting to turn out badly for them. There are angry comments on Facebook: "Hamas has attacked people for no reason at all, they beat them and showered outrageous insults on them."

The left-wingers and the human rights movements are

not the only ones to express their indignation, some of the more liberal Hamas leaders joined in as well. The officer and his henchmen try to defend themselves by saying, "It wasn't us."

"Of course it was you. I saw with my own eyes attackers dressed in pajamas come back to take refuge here. I can testify to that."

"No, you can't. You're the ones who are responsible."

"Us? You claim that we were stabbing each other? But it was you who stabbed my friend."

He doesn't know what to say. He's silent for a moment, then he says, "I must warn you that it's not your father who will come to collect you. We've decided that it's the family mayor who will take you out of here."

The family mayor is one of my uncles, a brother of my mother, but he has to come from Rafah, a journey that takes an hour and a half. He's conservative, but he does love me a lot. He's very much like his father, my Grandfather Abdullah, which makes me feel weak when facing him, I can't refuse him anything. I've never forgotten how good he's always been to me. When he comes into the prison he's accompanied by his brother, my Uncle Ahmed, whose library made me dream so much. They sit down at a table and Officer Tayeb starts to scold them, "If I'd found out that my daughter smoked, I'd have killed her."

We all remain silent, then my uncle says to me, "Come on, we're going."

"Yes, but I'm not going to sign any documents."

Tayeb literally goes crazy. "If you go on talking like that, you'll remain under lock and key. Even if day turns into night, I won't release you."

"As for me, I don't want to get out. I'm staying in prison."

Uncle Ahmed doesn't say anything, he can't bring himself to tell me to do this or that. But my other uncle, the mayor, starts crying. He's wearing my grandfather's *'abaya*, he has his skullcap on. Head lowered, he lets the tears run down in silence. It makes me feel terribly upset. "I'll sign anything you want," I say. "I just want to get out of here."

Officer Tayeb explodes with rage, "I don't want you to sign anything at all anymore! Get out!"

We went out, my two uncles and I, and walked. I can remember that we spoke on the way, but I no longer know what about. At home we continued to talk, even to laugh. I was shattered but strangely happy. My father said to my uncle, "From now on your official function will be to get Asmaa out of prison," and everyone burst out laughing. The next day the journalists flocked to the house, and the press union and foreigners, a crazy mob. I was deathly pale, I was wracked with pain on that second day, I was completely done. As for Sameh, she was lying on a couch at home, making every effort to recover from the stabbing wound she'd received.

My maternal uncle passed on a message from my Uncle Saïd to me, "If you had insisted on staying in prison, they could have killed you. They'll certainly get you if you write anything else." I said to the messenger, "Tell my Uncle Saïd to keep his mouth shut if he wants to stop me publishing another article on him." I know that my message was passed on to him because he actually did remain silent from then on.

Some Hamas policemen set up outside our house, I realized I no longer had the right to go out. But that wasn't the end of the story, the Palestinian Spring still had a few more tricks up its sleeve. Ten or so brave friends managed to find a way of getting into the UNRWA offices and starting a sit-in there. As I had to stay shut in at home, I went up onto the roof to observe the apartment block they were occupying, which was quite near. I managed to make contact with them through some mutual friends' Twitter accounts. Other friends used the same tactic and occupied the office of the UNDB, the United Nations' development program. But in their cowardly way the U.N. asked both to leave—and the young people were savagely beaten by Hamas officers as they left. Slightly embarrassed, the UNRWA published a press release protesting its neutrality. My father then published a letter to his brother Saïd that I reproduced on my blog: "What is it you want? Leave my children in peace." The letter made quite a stir, but the Palestinian Spring stopped there... at least for the moment.

27

Why Pierce Her Ears?

COMING BACK FROM SERBIA, where I'd taken part in a colloquium, I spent a night in Cairo. It was April 15, 2011. When I woke up, there was a message on my cell: "The forces of the Palestine resistance condemn the assassination of Vittorio Arrigoni." It sent me out of my mind. Vittorio was an Italian activist who'd been settled in Gaza since 2008, a friend! I immediately called a journalist colleague, he was in tears. "They kidnapped him and killed him," he said. Who? A small Salafi organization called Tawhid wa Jihad ('Unity and Jihad') which had been demanding the release of their leader, imprisoned by Hamas one month previously, in exchange for Vittorio. Dissident Islamists! Hamas still had a monopoly of power, but there was something festering in the Islamist world; fratricidal feelings were running high leading to internal violence—and it was my Italian friend who was paying for it.

Oh, Vittorio! He and I were always arguing, but didn't we laugh at the same time! He would wander around Gaza showing off his tattoos, he smoked a pipe and sometimes disguised himself to make us laugh. At times, I thought he was as naive as the other pacifist left-wingers who believed they could discern a certain 'purity' in Hamas. He used to say that he wasn't bothered about the differences between the rival organizations, the only important thing for him was Palestine as a whole. But he had come to the March 15 demonstration, which was implicitly directed against Hamas. He was one of us, I didn't speak to him as if he was a foreigner.

At the Rafah border I ran into Teresa, his fiancée, who was also desperate to get back to Gaza as quickly as possible. I took her hands in mine, and we hired a taxi together; she cried the whole way. When we arrived, the Foreign Ministry had arranged an official reception for her—Hamas wanted to show that it had nothing to do with the nasty business, which it condemned. The Minister's representative took us in his car, accompanying me home and taking Teresa to some friends where she was to spend the night. One hour later, we were all with her for a vigil in memory of Antonio; the organizers were the same people who had called for the March 15 rally. The next day, as we were preparing to throw rice on the coffin during the funeral—a Lebanese tradition—a security officer came over and whispered in my ear, "Hey you, listen. Don't throw any rice."

"Why not?"

"I'm telling you, don't throw a single grain of rice."

I could see from his eyes how much Hamas detested me. So I gave the rice I'd prepared to various people, asking them to throw it for me, and the flowers as well. The mortuary was packed. Amid all the tears there was a great outcry when Vittorio's body was taken out of the cold room.

I wrote an article on the assassination that was translated into Italian; there were a lot of responses because Vittorio was well-known in Italy. In it I mentioned the threats he'd had before he was kidnapped and which he'd refused to take seriously. After I'd sent the article off, I realized that the threats were very similar to the ones sent to me: the same words, the same curses, the same turns of phrase. Suddenly I was very afraid. And once again the police refused to record my complaint. I then decided to report the police to the human rights organizations—but that didn't get me anywhere either. Whether the threats came from the same group that had assassinated Vittorio or from some other organization in the Islamist constellation, I had no protection at all—and it wasn't the security service that was going to give me some. I felt defenseless, I didn't even dare introduce myself under my own name anymore... *Asmaa*, it's the plural of *ism*, which means: name. So therefore I'm called... names. Consequently I have no special name, I'm a multitude of them. That name has sometimes been a blessing, sometimes a disaster. In reality, I'm braver than myself. I said to my father, to my mother, even to the police officer, "It's over, I've stopped campaigning"—and I was out in the streets again the very next day. I couldn't stop myself. There's something inside me that impels me to go and demonstrate, something that makes me write the way I write. But if up to then I'd felt free to do as I pleased, it was because there was no one I had to be afraid for. By this time I had a son of seven. I told myself I had to protect him and give my parents some respite. So I decided to leave Gaza and settle in Egypt for a few months.

In Cairo, I had a delightful friend called Mahmoud. There was an uncommon gentleness in his gestures, in his hands. One evening, I came across him sitting at a table in a café with some friends and we started to chat. After a while, one of his friends got up and left. Mahmoud said, "Oh, Tamer's forgotten his cigarettes."

"Oh, that's Tamer is it?"

"Yes."

"Next time, introduce him to me."

That was because for some time I'd been hearing about Tamer: translator, poet and a militant with the Egyptian Spring. He came back having gotten his cigarettes.

"You're Tamer?"

"And you're Asmaa?"

We exchanged telephone numbers. Three weeks later he asked me if I would marry him, which amazed me: usually men are afraid of me, as always, I'm "too strong-minded"— which I interpret as meaning "difficult to dominate." So I was grateful to him for his courage, even if I was wary of certain differences of opinion that I sensed. My father came to Cairo and Tamer officially asked him for my hand in marriage. Mahmoud was the witness at our wedding, of course. I already knew that Tamer disapproved of the way I dressed and spoke, but I felt safe with him, in my eyes he represented the traditional man. To be absolutely honest, I was tired of Gaza, I needed a refuge and I thought marriage would give me the necessary protection, and Tamer seemed to be the man for that. That is the paradox that I am: I want a man who doesn't clip my wings yet is capable of defending me. With the Arab world the way it is, I dreamed of the rare bird that would protect me and at the same time protect my freedom—squaring the circle! It wasn't long before problems arose. It was my fault. My fantasy of being a 'normal' woman leading a 'normal' life with a 'normal' man naturally fell apart. I decided to give up my blog. As a farewell I posted one last text: "The love of Gaza." I also closed my Twitter account and went back to my country. I was pregnant. My stay in Egypt had lasted eight long months.

The assassination of Vittorio Arrigoni had changed a lot of things in Gaza. Firstly Hamas had decreed that from now on we were forbidden to mix with foreigners: no more parties, no more meetings, nothing. After that, the repression imposed on us intensified to the point where it led to further departures. One leader of the Young Folk of March 15 and two founders of the GYBO had left, the first for Egypt, the other for Qatar, the third went I don't know where... My friend May, with whom I went through the 'beach affair' had packed up and gone to Spain, another pal had chosen Belgium. There was no one left! Anyone who is subject to oppression has the right to leave. But why do they do it? They are victims because they wanted to change things, not so as to become political refugees. That's my opinion—but I don't have the right to judge others.

One month later Tamer followed me to Gaza and, against all expectation, our reunion was marvelous. My belly was starting to swell properly. On the other hand, my work wasn't going very well. My mother had secretly sold her gold bracelet to pay for the birth. I took Tamer to all the places I loved, to Rafah, to the fish restaurants, to the beach, everywhere. He was delighted, we had a wonderful time. We talked about my pregnancy, about Zeina who was going to arrive soon... The day before he left we went to the flea-market to buy presents for his parents and also some olive oil—much better than in Egypt. He came back to Gaza when I was in my seventh month, and our happiness was the same. We were content whatever should happen, I was working hard, we lived in a room in my parents' house but that didn't bother us. Everything was fine. He then came back again in June 2012 for the birth. It was the end of Ramadan. As soon as he arrived we sat down to break our fast. Then Tamer went to pray in the next room and the telephone rang. My brother Abdullah said, his voice cracking, "Mahmoud's dead."

"How did it happen?"

"He went for a swim in the sea, he drowned."

I went to find Tamer, asked him to sit down, held his hands and told him the sad news—Mahmoud was his best friend, the witness at our marriage... He started to cry, we fell into each others' arms and cried together. But from that moment on, he became a different person and I still haven't understood why. He started to look at me as if I were the one who had killed Mahmoud. We managed to get by, one way or another, because I was still working for *Skeyes*. Fortunately I was awarded the American prize for Courage in Journalism when Zeina was almost three months old. I was invited to accept it in the United States. I could go there with my daughter, but I insisted that Tamer was also invited.

So we went to Egypt to take the plane. Tamer's family in Cairo was happy because the invitation made it possible for him to visit his brothers who lived over in the States. At dinner we happened to be talking about the necessity of having Zeina's ears pierced so that she would be able to wear earrings. One of Tamer's nephews, who was fifteen, said, "But why pierce her ears? She's going to be veiled anyway and her ears won't be visible."

"But how do you know she's going to put on a veil?" I asked.

"Her father and her brother will decide that," the boy replied.

"Why? You think she'll have no say in the matter?" During the whole time this discussion was going on, Tamer was looking at me as if he wanted to strangle me. He—the poet, the militant of the Egyptian Spring—was ashamed of everything I said. I was talking about *his* daughter. I will never forget that terrifying look. I realized I had landed in a disaster zone and that Zeina was certainly going to have a difficult future.

In America I realized to what extent I had regressed: my intellectual level, my confidence, my courage... everything had gone. I had become timid, ill-at-ease, counting the days until it was over. I stopped liking the United States because of him. His brother Brahim detested me; he pretended to know Gaza and its inhabitants and made stupid remarks to which I stopped replying. One day I said to Tamer, "Listen, I sense that a new war is going to break out: all the things that happened before the conflict of 2008 are happening again. We have to go back."

He didn't believe me, he wanted to stay. At the moment we said goodbye, he started to cry and I returned to Gaza alone, with my daughter. Four days later, on November 14, 2012, Ahmed Jabari, the head of Hamas military operations, was killed in an Israeli raid. A new war had started.

28

And Death Will Go with You

THE ISRAELI ARMY didn't invade the country; it restricted itself to bombarding it from all sides at once—land, sea and air. The din never stopped, it was a terrible rumbling that threatened to burst your eardrums. It was the F16s in particular, which launched bombs and missiles that literally terrified me, though I couldn't say why—I had lived through similar bombardments during the war of 2008 without feeling afraid. Four years later, the explosions made me start with fright, I would pick up Zeina and tell myself, "My daughter's learning about fear when she's only four months old." It would certainly have been easier if I'd been working—the 'mission' of journalism gives you a kind of illusion of a shield—but there was no longer a newspaper that would employ me. Was it my reputation as a troublemaker? Was it my marriage, my problems with Tamer and my pregnancy that had made me lose contact? Whatever, the fact is that I'd offered my services to various newspapers and they hadn't even bothered to reply.

So I went outside to check out what was happening and wrote on my Facebook page every evening. The number of my followers was constantly growing, but it still wasn't the same. I was afraid all the time, out in the street, in the car, everywhere... afraid of death especially. It wasn't so much the physical fear but rather the *idea* of death which accompanied me everywhere. Two journalists had been killed during the first days of the war. They were members of Hamas, but so what? They were still journalists and civilians. They were driving down a street and a bomb had pulverized their car. What is it, the moment of death? Do you become 'absent' from one second to the next, do you die without knowing you're dead? These questions would go around and around inside my head and I trembled. I was in a car as well, incapable of controlling my trembling. Throughout his life Papa used to say to us, "I'm going to die," as a joke. When I was little I was frightened that he might die, and I thought about death, but I had still never felt it so close. The two pieces I wrote on my Facebook page on death, its closeness, its mystery brought two hundred comments.

When Jabari was killed, the press naturally focused its attention on the event that had set off the war, but my attention was attracted by much less spectacular details. For example, a drama that had taken place that same day: a little girl is sitting on her mother's knee in a parlor where visitors are about to leave. The bombardment starts the moment they go out. The mother hurries to put her other children in a less exposed place and returns for her daughter. At that very moment a bomb falls and destroys the parlor: "I see my daughter unharmed, sitting where I'd left her, there's nothing obvious wrong with her, not a drop of blood... but she's dead." That story made a deep impression on me. It reminded me of a boy who was supposed to come home from school during the 2008 war and whom his parents had waited for in vain. They left no stone unturned, they went around to all the hospitals and the morgues without finding any trace of him. In the evening they saw him at the foot of a wall, his satchel on his back, absolutely intact. A tiny piece of shrapnel had penetrated his heart but nothing could be seen. These dead children, these little girls that are taken out of morgue fridge with a barrette in their hair... I would see my own children in them. It made my blood freeze. Someone told me the story of a paramedic who didn't feel the explosion of the shell that hit him in the back: he was helping wounded people up and suddenly lay down to join them. The words "barbarity" or "massacres" seem like inadequate clichés to describe events like that. Such a level of reality is simply impossible to express. How can you put into words our familiarity with the feeling of death within us, the intimacy we share with it?

Fernando Eichenberg, a Brazilian journalist, called me; it was the first time he'd come to Gaza. "All the hotels are full. I've found a room where I can stay, the translator who rents it is asking three hundred dollars for it."

I asked him to wait a second and went to see my father. "I have a foreign journalist on the line. Can we put him up in the house?"

"Of course. It has the blessing of religion, the Koran itself recommends it."

Our house was full to bursting: my brothers and sisters, my parents, my sister's son, my children... The journalist came to live with us, and I accompanied him every day. I interpreted for him, but I refused to accept a dime. He never knew how broke I was. He bought oriental pastries and toys for the children. No one had had any idea how he was going to make the war easier for all of us.

My son and my nephew became very attached to him, they called him "uncle." We ate together, we went to the war together. My sister, who was studying architecture and was keen to improve her English, started going out with us as well. A friend took us out in his car, and we were frightened to death every day. And everything that happened to us was there on my Facebook page in the evening. Marvelous days! But also, sometimes, terrible nights. When the bombardment came closer and the din threw us down on the floor, our journalist friend was quivering with fear. Then Papa would say to him, "Come over here and be with us." And we were all there on the floor, my little nephew with his hair all sticking up and my son Nasser, Zeina in her cot and all of us terrified. Taking advantage of a lull, we all went to the supermarket to unwind. We filled the cart to the rim before going home and stuffing ourselves with bulimic appetites.

One minute before the end of the war, just one minute, the Israeli army bombarded a tower-block that was so close to our house that I could hear the sound of the broken windows falling onto the road. A voice suddenly started shouting, "A martyr! A martyr!" and I was shouting, "A bombardment! A bombardment!" We went out on to the balcony to have a look. Guessing what was about to happen, Mama locked the house door to stop us going out. Fernando had to go out to work, me too. He asked her to open the door, she said no. He begged her, she held the key behind her back and made it impossible for him to get it. At the same time we were all laughing! I ran out onto the balcony to take some photos on my phone, then came back inside where Fernando and Mama were still confronting each other. Eventually she agreed to open the door, and we went out. There we heard that it wasn't a haphazard bombardment but a 'personal' missile that had gone in through a window. At the same time another missile had executed one of the Hamas leaders in another part of the town: death at the last minute. After that final twist, the war finished and Fernando left.

29

Reconciliation with My Uncle

"THIS IS THE ONLINE NEWSPAPER *Al Monitor,* we would like you to write for us."

I made a cautious reply, "I can't hear you very well, send me an email."

They did so, they seemed serious. Their site, specializing on the Middle East, is hosted from the United States with correspondents in the Arab world, in Israel, in Turkey, in Iran... The next day I wrote an article for them about the Christians' Christmas in Gaza, then another on rap in the territory, which they also published. All they asked was for me to make my articles shorter—I had lost the habit of restricting myself—but everything I sent was published immediately, both in Arabic and English. I started writing again every day—with a certain sense of jubilation, for the first time in a long while I felt I was valued as a journalist again.

Tamer came back to Cairo—he'd ended up spending six months in the United States. I begged him to come back to Gaza, I didn't want to live without him any longer. He had made me suffer, true, but what could I do? At the very beginning we'd decided to live in Gaza, that was our agreement, and I certainly hadn't married him in order to live by myself. I went to see him in Egypt, and we left for Alexandria together. For two days he was pleasant and thoughtful, and I was happy as I boarded the plane for Oslo, where I was going to take part in a colloquium. Oddly enough, I didn't like the talk I gave there at all, I'd lost some of my forcefulness as a speaker. What had happened? Was it because of my more or less avowed desire to be a wife who avoids attracting trouble? Was it my new work impelling me to observe greater neutrality toward Hamas and Fatah or anyone else? Was I in the process of moving away from the clear positions I had adopted?

In December 2012, the managing director of the online newspaper called to offer me a permanent contract, which I accepted with pleasure. Now I was a columnist for *Al Monitor*, and in that capacity I increased the number of interviews with the Hamas leaders, who were now obliged to talk to me—I, who had vilified them in such a cruel manner. I even became a friend of one of them, a person whose mind worked at top speed—doubtless because he came from the Popular Front. He introduced me to his wife, a remarkable woman who worked for an international organization and never stopped criticizing Hamas. And one day my Uncle Saïd went past as I was conducting an interview outside an apartment block in Rafah with a team from Dutch TV. He walked past and stopped for a moment before turning back. He came to greet me and suddenly hugged me. That was how we became reconciled with each other, without a single word. Neither about the past nor about the events that had separated us. My father's different, he's not the kind of person to hide his feelings, he's always talking—in fact that's the first thing he did when he came back from his long sulk in Rafah. We're a family that *talks* nonstop. On every birthday—and we have them right through the year given the size of the family—he asks the one who is celebrating to say a few words. My Uncle Saïd is more taciturn. When I saw him again he still had the same position with Hamas, and I was still writing whatever

I wanted to. Our reconciliation was strictly a family matter—politics is different. We'd spent six years not saying a single word to each other! One day during that long period I'd come home without being expected and found him there; he'd come to say hello to my father. He'd been surprised to see me.

I'd greeted him politely, then added, "So you're still torturing your prisoners?"

"We don't torture them, we give them chicken with rice..."

"You do? In that case I'm sure you order it from the Maatouk (a well-known restaurant)."

The atmosphere was electric, and we stopped there. As he was leaving, he turned to me and said, "By the way, I'm the one who's stopping them from harming you... They want to kill you."

"Why do you do that? Kill me, that'll be better, my voice will be all the stronger!"

My father didn't know how to stop us. But I'm not particularly proud of my opposition to my uncle or to Hamas. When I look back I see that I've been a disaster for myself, my parents, my friends—and I have no idea what kind of people Nasser and Zeina will become after the childhood they've had. What mother has a prison visit from her son of five? Every time he hears a demo go past, Nasser panics and asks, "Are you going out, Mama?" And when the people from Hamas turn up, he runs over to me, terrified. "Mama, it's Hamas..." And I say, "Don't worry, they're not coming for me."

Despite all that, or perhaps precisely because of it, my son started to love Hamas when he was nine. He told me how he intended to join it, put photos of its fighters on his computer screen, listened to their songs. I realized that a certain image had formed in his eyes, just as one had appeared in mine when I was little: that is that the 'resistance fighters' were there to defend us. They sent us an image of strength and power at a time when we seemed wretched and destitute. Moreover, during the second war, that of 2012, Hamas had drawn lessons from the mistakes they'd made in the previous one: this time they looked after people, they'd arranged for emergency services and hadn't attacked their Fatah rivals. Thus they'd managed to give the impression that a rocket launched against Israel was precisely what was defending us—more than the U.N., Hillary Clinton, France or Europe. In the eyes of the people of Gaza, Israel had been stupid enough to make Hamas look like a resistance movement rather than an oppressive regime. And that regime came out of the war relatively popular, despite all the suffering and destruction.

As I could see what was going on inside my son's head, I didn't oppose him, quite the opposite. "Nasser," I said, "if you want to meet someone from Hamas you can do so."

He asked me if he could go and watch a military parade of the Al Qassam Brigades, and I took him. If I'd wanted to persuade him not to, what could I have said that he didn't already know? He'd seen me arrested, imprisoned and beaten by Hamas, there was nothing new I could tell him. He had to think for himself, and I let him go ahead. The attraction Hamas held for him disappeared of its own accord, and that fairly quickly. I had invited him to go to Spain with me, where he watched a soccer match with Barcelona in the Camp Nou, one of the biggest stadiums in the world. He came out dazzled—but without, for all that, dreaming of becoming a soccer player. Perhaps he sensed that day that there was more than just Hamas and that a different future was possible.

He asked me, "Why do I have to learn Arabic, Mama?"

"But... why do you ask?"

"Because I want to learn the science of insects in English."

That was his latest idea, to devote himself to insects, to

spend his life doing that. He'd managed to go back to an inclination he'd always had: the attraction that animal life held for him.

30

The Secret Life of Gaza

O N JUNE 30, 2013, the famous slogan of the Arab Spring once more rang out in the Egyptian streets: "The people want the fall of the regime!" Thousands of demonstrators, worn down by poverty and insecurity, came together to demonstrate in Cairo and the large towns of the country. But this time it was the dismissal of Mohamed Morsi that was being demanded, the first president elected by a democratic vote that the Egyptian Spring itself had imposed. This spectacular reversal was to have a fatal effect on the situation in Gaza: Morsi was in power in the name of the Muslim Brotherhood, the organization that had given birth, among others, to the Palestinian Hamas.

Despite my loathing of the Islamists, I think I would have voted for him the previous year if I had been Egyptian: at least he had come from a revolution that had thrown down Mubarak's military dictatorship by an election. Three weeks before the great demonstration there was a persistent rumor going around in Gaza to the effect that Egypt "was going to get rid of Morsi and the Muslim Brotherhood" before the end of the month. I had called Tamer in Cairo and warned him, and he'd replied, "Don't believe those rumors, nothing's going to happen." In reality, the regime of the Muslim Brotherhood had turned out to be so incompetent that the people rose against it. The tidal wave was so impressive that

I wrote on my Facebook page, "I bow before this revolution." But it wasn't a revolution, just a sham very well orchestrated by the high command of the Egyptian army. As soon as I realized that, I wrote that it was a disguised military coup d'état that was causing hundreds of deaths. At once I was assailed by attacks of rare violence. What was it I'd said? I immediately lost a lot of my friends, colleagues turned their backs on me, people I loved didn't say a word to me anymore. They told me my stance was playing into the hands of Hamas. Voices that agreed with me were rare. And Tamer, who had moved closer to the Islamists, talked to me from Cairo in a mildly ironic tone, "You've always opposed Hamas and now it's become 'good' to be with the Muslim Brotherhood?"

"This has nothing to do with it being 'good'. You just don't understand. I've been like that all my life, but you've never paid attention."

In fact, he was looking on me with respect for the first time in ages, but he was mistaken. He didn't understand that I was acting for democracy and out of hatred of massacres. Some thought that it was him who had influenced me. Others claimed I had taken up that position because I was working for *Al Monitor*, an American site which maintained that it was a coup d'état. Everyone had their own little explanation. In fact, however, the position I took up was one of principle, that's all—as was that of my father, moreover. My sister, who lived in Egypt and was more of a communist, had seen most of her Facebook friends oppose the military. Like me, like everyone with a sense of honor. But in Gaza very few could understand that one could denounce both a military regime and an Islamist regime at the same time. Hamas itself started singing my praises, and I refused to put up with that.

I wrote on the Facebook page of a friend who belonged to Hamas and had shared my first office, "Hamas and you are the last people who can say I'm on the right side... I've always been against you and still am, nothing has changed. I haven't forgotten how you called me a mercenary, a liar... And now you think me 'good' because I'm taking a stand for the Brotherhood? But I'm not taking a stand for the Brotherhood. I'm simply for what is right, and the Muslim Brotherhood has nothing to do with it."

The fall of Morsi was a terrible blow for Hamas, who had relied on the 'friendly regime' of the Brotherhood to keep open the thousands of tunnels under the border with Egypt, which ensured that supplies could reach the territory (including their own military 'imports'). At the same time they had fallen out with their other great ally, the Iranian government, whom it was criticizing for its support for Bashar al-Assad's Syrian government. In a word, Hamas' political line had brought Gaza to the point of asphyxia. Israeli products were still prohibitively expensive, and the destruction of the tunnels with Egypt sent prices soaring. Sugar, which had been at 3 shekels a kilo, rose to 7. We stopped buying cheese and forgot about powdered milk. In simple terms: groceries started costing the equivalent of $400 a month. Previously, rent was around $160-200 a month, now you couldn't find anything under $300! We had power outages lasting twelve hours a day. Because they could no longer find places to stay, people starting living together more and more, in extended families. They had already been doing that, but not to such an extent. When a couple got married the family would give them—if it was possible—a room in their shared apartment. At the University, every class had to use the books of the preceding one because no books were coming into Gaza anymore. We had to live in that confinement, on top of each other, with all those restrictions, in a society that was eating itself up, immersed in the perpetual zzzz of the Israeli drones. But you still had to get up in the morning to take the children to school, do the shopping and the cooking, go to work and write, witness death and learn how to die. This bitter reality gives birth to terrible ideologies, it gives the Islamists wings.

And yet in a certain way, everything mysteriously continued to hold together. Even though the official unemployment figures remained very high, there weren't many people out of work. A number of Gazans—primary- and secondary-school teachers, doctors, etc.—were paid directly by the UNRWA. The salaries of those who worked in the private sector—institutions, universities, banks—or for NGOs, etc., came from outside. Thirty-two thousand civil servants refused to work with Hamas and therefore stayed at home while the Palestinian Authority—Fatah—continued to pay their salaries. But how were they going to ask these Fatah civil servants—men and women used to sitting idly in their parlors since 2007—to go back to work when the day came? And, anyway, some had emigrated and applied for political asylum, claiming that Hamas had oppressed them. Thus they could get themselves paid by naive foreign governments while their salary continued to arrive in Gaza. During those days, the Hamas civil servants insulted the Islamist movement on Facebook because it didn't have enough money any longer to pay them and shut them up.

The citizens who didn't belong to any of these categories (workers, peasants, the unemployed, storekeepers, artists, graduates without work, etc.) were completely lost. A falafel sandwich, the cheapest meal in Gaza, which used to cost a half-shekel, now cost two. And all that without mentioning the other problems: the pollution, the constructions going ahead without a master plan, without town planning, the illnesses that were spreading; for example, cancer, the numbers of which increased rapidly because of Israel's use of depleted uranium shells, as was established by the report of the South African Judge Goldstone, the official investigator appointed by the United Nations.

Despite all of this, people continued to laugh in Gaza. When the Israeli drones came too close they jammed television reception and stopped people receiving the *Al Jazeera* channel, for example. When we were prevented from viewing an important soccer match or a TV series in the evening, we would shout insults at Israel and our own government. Television is the thing that gives the most pleasure in Gaza. The water to give yourself a shower was off, there was no electricity for a regular Internet connection, but what did that matter, we had the television. And if there was a power cut, a car battery was enough to get it working. I used to go and visit a child who had lost his sight when his house was bombarded. He was an extraordinary kid. As I went in that evening I saw him riding a bicycle, even though he was blind. He recognized me from my voice. He couldn't see a thing, his house was half destroyed, his parents had nothing to eat... but what were they doing? They were delightedly watching— on a flat-screen TV taking up half of one of the walls—a Turkish series set in a richly furnished lounge!

These series are incredibly successful. In them people see characters that are like themselves, Muslims who read the Koran, pray and fast... and drink alcohol, go out with girls in short dresses and sleep with them. They are like us, but not like us. The Turkish series show neither a possible goal in life nor a possible way of life but are a kind of virtual compensation for the intellectual and religious state of siege, for the flagrant absence of freedoms. Whatever the situation, the TV never stops working in Gaza, just like sex—between married couples, of course. It's an extraordinary country. Women of all kinds, including those veiled up to their eyes, spend their time in shops buying new nightdresses and thongs. That's Gaza, the secret life of Gaza.

31

The Arab Idol

MOHAMED ASSAF was twenty years old. He'd grown up in fairly modest surroundings in Khan Younis, at the southern end of the Gaza Strip. His father was a civil servant and his mother a teacher. He had a beautiful voice and charged 600 shekels—the equivalent of $150—to entertain at parties, weddings, celebrations... In 2013, he took part in the "Arab Idol" competition, a talent show with competitors from all over the Arab world, a significant annual event.

Gaza was swollen with pride. Suddenly one of its sons was appearing in the limelight: a singer with a golden voice who could sing using all the different accents of the Arab world. The way it worked was that you had to vote for the competitors using your cell phone—which, obviously, devoured the credit of your phonecard. I was stone broke back then, yet I spent the equivalent of hundreds of dollars to take part in the vote—also by lending my phone to those who were even worse off than I was.

There was an incredible sense of solidarity in the territory, orchestrated via Facebook and the other social networks. Mohamed Assaf had to go to Alexandria to take part in the contest. But we were in Gaza, and the border with Egypt was closed. It took him two days to cross it! And when he reached the gates of the grounds of the Grand Hotel in Alexandria, where the competition was to take place, he found them closed. So he telephoned his mother to explain that he was locked out.

She replied, "Jump over the wall."

"But how can I, Mama?"

"Jump, I tell you."

He jumped. On the other side the dogs came rushing over toward him, followed by security guards.

"I've come from Gaza to take part in the 'Arab Idol' competition," he told them.

"It's too late for you. All the numbers have been given out to the participants, you can't enter it now."

Another young Palestinian, who had come from the Emirates and heard this conversation, said, "Here, take my number."

And that's how Mohamed Assaf managed to get into the great hall. Later, after having gone through a number of rounds, he found himself in the final, facing one male and one female singer, and the whole of Palestine was holding its breath. In the heart of the wretched refugee camp of Nuseirat, in the middle of the Gaza Strip, a hundred people were waiting for the result in a beach café. On the screen the presenter was taking her time: "And the winner is..." Unable to bear it any longer, one of the men in the café burst out with, "Oh fuck off! Come on, tell us!"—and she announced the victory of Mohamed Assaf! The scene at the café, filmed on a cell phone and posted on Facebook, has been shared thousands of times.

The explosion of joy was indescribable, the whole of Palestine was out in the streets. In Nablus the viewers gathered together in a stadium with a giant screen went wild and smashed all the seats in the stadium—with joy! In the city of Gaza, Hamas had banned gatherings, with the result that people were crammed together around TV screens in hotels and cafés. When the result was announced, the men and women got up and started to dance together for the first time in their lives while the TV cameras filmed them. I was also watching on the small screen, but at home with my family. I must have jumped up and down at least twenty times, laughing and crying at the same time. Under the spotlights the great victor held out his hand to invite the young Palestinian who had given him his number to come up on stage and sing the last song with him. Not only had Mohamed Assaf won, he had received 80 million votes while the one who was second only got 40! It was the greatest number of votes and the greatest difference ever recorded during the existence of "Arab Idol."

He has handsome, dark-haired and slim—all the girls were crazy about him. We knew he was liberal, close to the Popular Front. Hamas was said to have arrested and beaten him four or five times. He was our brother! The government didn't say a single word after his triumph. Everyone knew that well before becoming successful, Mohamed Assaf had had problems for having sung a 'forbidden' song, *Lift High the Keffiah,* that was seen as favoring Fatah. However the Hamas government did, after all, send an official delegation to welcome him at the border. Hundreds of thousands of overexcited people were waiting for him—to the point where he couldn't get out of the car. He was criticized for that, but I can understand why: God knows what would have happened if he had gotten out. All the same he could have made a detour to the refugee camp where he was born before going to the seven-star hotel where he was expected.

In the Gaza mosques people started to hear negative sermons about him: his behavior was *haram* and he himself was a *kafir,* an unbeliever... But people didn't support that denigration. Their need for a national symbol they could be proud of was so great that they silenced the sheikhs by insulting them. For once, we had a talented man to show the world rather than our wars or our destitution.

I read a story that made a great impression on me. It was about a young man from the West Bank who had thrown a Molotov cocktail at a vehicle coming out of an Israeli settlement. The home-made mixture had bounced on the hood without igniting. The car stopped and a woman got out, a British woman who was a teacher at the University. She walked over to the young man and asked him, "Why did you throw a Molotov cocktail at me?"

The kid didn't know what to say. They exchanged addresses. And when he'd finished his studies on the West Bank, she helped him enroll in an American university, where he was a brilliant success. He wrote to her, "You, my mother, whom I got to know by chance and who have saved me..." That encapsulates the whole dilemma of Palestinians: either they choose the Molotov cocktail or sometimes a fortuitous event puts them on a path that allows them to discover their gifts. Such is the story of Mohamed Assaf and of this young man. Our societies, alas, are constructed in such a way as to kill off talent when it's so easy to make a Molotov cocktail.

My brother Abdullah decided to go back and live in our house in Rafah for a while to write the script on which he was working. He met several of my cousins who were still living there. He was always asking them, "What is your aim in life?" One day one of these cousins, who detested me, called me. He wasn't a child, he was twenty-seven. "I'm in Gaza and I don't know where to go, could I come to your place?"

I was very surprised. That cousin was a member of the Al Qassam brigades. Despite that, I told him to come.

"I've discovered some important things, Asmaa."

"What?"

"I've discovered you, your blog, why you did the things

you did, a whole new world. Previously, when I was listening to a song on the radio, my aunt would say to my mother, 'Your son is corrupt, he's dirty.' Now I watch films, I read books and I've come to understand that if my sister says, 'I love someone,' I don't need to go and beat him up. Where have we been all this time?"

I couldn't get over it.

He went on, "When your brother Abdullah came to Rafah, he spoke to me and I realized I didn't know the world."

I laughed. "You still have a lot to learn," I told him. I made some coffee and we went on talking. I thought a lot about this story. I realized to what extent books, the cinema, music, all these important things, were alien to the children of Gaza. But they are the things that can transform people, just as they transformed me. How can one judge those who've never had access to them? There's not a single public cinema in the whole territory! In general, young people have just one choice: either get stoned on Tramadol or join the Al Qassam brigades, become soldiers. Any other choice only comes to them by accident—because they have a beautiful voice, because a woman they don't know bawls them out, because a cousin talks to them, or because their father is different. It is a choice that God unfortunately doesn't send down from Heaven. That was when I came to understand that there's only a hair's-breadth distance between ending up as a professor/writer/poet or being a warrior and assassinating your sister in the belief that you're defending the family honor. This criminal conservatism is founded on illusions, fantasies, the slogans of the Party, the mosque, the government. But if you look inside someone, what do you see? All they need is a good book. That's what's needed in Gaza, nothing else. Neither a government of national unity, nor reconciliation, nor shit, nor Hamas, nor war. All that this territory needs is to be opened up to the world, and it's the siege imposed by Israel, Hamas, Fatah and Egypt that forbids it—while the United States and Europe look the other way.

All the films shown in Gaza, except for those at the French Institute, are supposed to be viewed in advance by Hamas. In a 2010 festival with the pretty name of "In the Eyes of Women" the Islamist organization had demanded (and obtained) that a sequence showing two birds mating be cut... Morality in Gaza had had a narrow escape.

32

Death Comes Unannounced

I CAN REMEMBER the precise moment when the two preceding wars took me by surprise, but I simply can't remember the start of that of summer 2014. There was such a frenzy during the following days that it concealed the beginning. We lived through fifty-one days of terror, each one of which felt like the first. Death came unannounced, without asking how you felt about it, one second and that was it. I went toward death, and death would have nothing to do with me.

I entered a room where a little boy had died, a pretty little boy dressed in pink without a drop of blood, I could still feel the life in him. Beside him were other bodies, women so pale, so calm, so strange. I went out. The families of the victims were crammed together in one room, A woman grabbed my arm, crying, "My son, my son!"

"Which one is your son?" I asked her.

"A little boy dressed in pink." And I, like an idiot, told her that I'd just seen him.

"But where is he? What's wrong with him?"

"He's dead."

Then she took her breasts in her hands and started to cry, "And these, who are they going to suckle now?"

She seized me by the throat and squeezed compulsively to strangle me—until those present made her let go. It was like a scene from a nightmare, and I was playing the part of the bad guy. I'd made the worst mistake of my life. The doctors gave her a sedative and criticized me severely. I apologized as best I could. As a mother I'd have preferred to know the truth at once, but that's just speaking for myself. It was her only son. I realized that I wasn't going to die that day—it's only the good who die, the others are always spared.

The thunder of the bombs was so violent that a woman who lived nearby came to hide in our house. She was quivering with fear, but once she was there she started to look at my uncle's daughters and ask about the possibility of an engagement for her young nephew... It was funny.

The bombardment seemed to have finished, I went out on the balcony and my father followed me. The neighboring block, that had been bombarded so often, was seven meters away from us. A missile suddenly flew past between the two buildings and I saw it go into an eighth-floor apartment before it exploded. The force of the blast and the burning heat almost blew us off the balcony. As if in slow motion I saw myself stretch out an arm to get back down on the floor while a greater force was pulling me out into the void. I managed to hold onto my father's arm, how could I forget that moment, and I didn't fly away. There was a high-pitched whine piercing my ears, as if my eardrums had burst. Feeling our way, we managed to get back in through the balcony door. The apartment was in total darkness, the air full of smoke and powder. You couldn't see anything. We heard shouts from a distant room: "Papa! Asmaa!" We made our way toward the shouts. I saw Nasser and Zeina motionless in a corner, lit by a tiny little lamp. There was also part of my uncle's family, and Mama, who was crying. I took her in my arms. I looked at my father, his eyes were staring. On the balcony, one meter from where we'd been standing, a concrete pillar had come crashing down. If we'd been in its path, we'd have been completely crushed. We were given another life on that day.

In the press office, which had electricity and had provided a space for me, the driver, who was called Hamed, sometimes made coffee for us. That morning I found him sitting on the corner of the sofa, idle. I said, "What's up, Hamed?" He stood up to put the coffee pot on the stove. He was looking at us with a certain intensity. He served the coffee and then went out. One hour later the photographer, whom he was to drive to the office, called us, sobbing, "Hamed's dead, his car was hit by a missile."

We couldn't believe it, called him a liar of a madman. I shouted, "That's just not possible! 'TV' is written in huge letters on the roof."

At the other end of the line the photographer sounded as if he was going out of his mind, "But it was him, I tell you. I saw it! He was cut in two." He started to wail and moan.

I finished my article on the death of Hamed and sent it off. Antoun Issa, the editor of the *Monitor*, wrote in reply, "I was devastated by your piece," and I knew that I'd managed to express what I felt. Below the article, published in Arabic and English, the threats multiplied. Most of those who attacked me thought I was making it up, was defaming Israel, such brutality was unknown in their land! But what was it they thought? That I was lying deliberately? They called me "George Orwell," as if I were writing fiction. One of the threats even said, "We want to see you in your grave."

In fact, every time criticism of Israel was published, especially on English-language sites with a certain reputation, there was a massive and immediate counter-attack—as if there were a battalion of Israeli students keeping an eye on things around the clock. In Gaza, every time someone attacked the Islamist movement in one way or another, every time we called for a demonstration, dozens of people would rise up and respond as one, insulting and threatening us.

The same mindset! That of powers that imagine they possess the truth and intend to silence any criticism.

I happened to be in a hospital when a vehicle had been pulverized by a missile not far away. I saw the victims brought in or, rather, the human remains. Among other parts there was a leg with a black sandal on. As I was in reception, the paramedics put everything down right in front of me. The smell of gasoline and blood mixed caught my throat, my body was gripped by totally involuntary tremors, which lasted until a doctor came and put his hand over my eyes. At that moment it was as if I'd woken up—I had been about to lose consciousness.

It was more than I could stand. I ran out and called my mother, I was crying, I couldn't stop. I couldn't even relate what I'd seen in *Al Monitor*. Death immediately in front of you and on a television are two completely different things. On the screen the pictures are shown in an ideological or political light, with a 'meaning' that, basically weakens the event and makes it more bearable. But when it happens before your very eyes, the event brings you back to the essentials, to war and peace, good and evil, people who fall because history demands it... It's no longer about Palestine or anything else, it's the *raw fact* that you have before you, flesh, blood, death, the sandal and the people who were still talking a second before they died...

That is much more terrifying, there's no rail, no simple interpretation you can hold on to. You see innocent people perish, your eyes believe what they see but your heart refuses to accept it. It's brutal. People don't die surrounded by their family, their loved ones, they don't say farewell, they don't realize they're on the point of death. They die without choice, without anything.

People around them start crying "Allahu Akbar!" as if that was going to make death easier to bear. But even those words, "Allahu Akbar," don't make anything easier, don't add anything, they have no influence at all. The question that comes to mind is, rather, "Where is God?" Where is He indeed? If there is justice, where is it? The Israelis are hard enemies who show no mercy. They claim they're only killing those they intend to kill, but I saw that they could kill anyone at all, could make a mistake not giving a damn that they'd made a mistake. And they did make a lot of mistakes during that war. And deliberately! Where is he, the God of Israel?

Hamed's body cut in two... I don't know why, but that image was to come back to me later when the Islamic State proudly exposed to the world the horrors and outrages it shamelessly commits. Honestly, what a region! Between Syria's Bashar al-Assad, who massacres his own people with barrels of powder dropped from planes, the Islamic State that puts all peoples that aren't like them to the sword and Israel that, in its hunt for Hamas, kills a great majority of civilians, including more than 500 children, we're done for. The one carries out assassinations to keep his family in power, the other in the name of a warped interpretation of Islam, the third in the name of a so-called promised land. And the missiles always fall on the same people, the small fry, those who sleep believing they're safe and sound, who have the misfortune to be in the wrong place at the wrong time, who haven't got the right religion, who make the coffee before going out... Basically everything turns around religion in this region. And all those who have the power to kill exercise that power as they see fit. War is war, it carries people off like a flood.

33

The Hannibal Protocol

THE TRUCE ANNOUNCED by Israel that would start at 8 a.m. on August 1, 2014, aroused a huge sense of relief: at last we would be able to breathe a little. My father decided to take advantage of it to go to the house in Rafah. He got up early and set off at 7:30 a.m. One hour later the news broke: an Israeli soldier had been abducted in a tunnel, in Rafah as it happened. At 9:30 a.m., when my father got there, all hell was let loose on the town. Deluded by the announcement of the truce, thousands of people had gone out to buy provisions when one of the most violent bombardments hit them unexpectedly: 40 people were killed that morning and 230 injured.

On Facebook everyone was telling me, "There's not a single journalist on the spot. You come from Rafah, you have to go there."

I didn't lack the desire to do that and I was very worried about my father, but I also knew that Israel had triggered what it called the "Hannibal Protocol," a procedure that allowed it to shoot at more or less anything that moved if an Israeli soldier had been abducted.

On the pretext of avoiding a repetition of the affair with Gilad Shalit, a soldier freed after five years in captivity in exchange for a thousand Palestinian prisoners, the army had given itself the right to set off an immediate deluge of fire, even if it meant killing the abducted soldier and every living thing over a wide surrounding area. Faced with strong criticism, especially from Amnesty International, which condemned it for "serious violations of international humanitarian law that might be a question of war crimes," the Israeli army was to give up the "Hannibal Protocol" in June 2016, two years after the war, blandly citing "professional, operational and ethical questions."

For a while, I really didn't know what to do. I hesitated, then finally stayed where I was. Waking up the next morning I remembered having had a nightmare but I couldn't remember what it was about. I said to my mother, "There's going to be a disaster. I have to go to Rafah to look for Papa." She was flabbergasted and told me that was madness and I should forget it. She sensed that something was going on when she saw me go out onto the porch for a quiet telephone call, but I swore I was only going to the office. In order to go with at least a minimum of security I needed to persuade some colleagues: a convoy of foreign correspondents would be a more politically sensitive target. But when I made my announcement in the foyer of the journalists' hotel, most of them slipped away—until the moment when the correspondent of the *New York Times* and his photographer agreed to come. Others then joined us—for example, the team of *Al Jazeera International*—after all, they couldn't let the competition go ahead alone.

So we squashed into four cars. The road was entirely deserted, and we were terrified. We had to follow the route along the shore, turn inland as far as Khan Younis and take a minor road from there. I told my colleague from the *New York Times*, "Whatever happens we must keep going, the others will feel obliged to follow us." However he didn't agree, so we stopped by the sea, and the discussion started while the airplanes were circling above us—they'd certainly spotted us. When we reached Khan Younis, we realized that the *Al Jazeera International* car had disappeared—they were too frightened. The *New York Times* driver gave me his bulletproof vest and his helmet—a real gentleman, but the vest weighed a ton. The three cars continued with six people in all. The stretch between Khan Younis and Rafah was the most dangerous. My colleagues wanted to stop once again, saying, "We can't just rely on God and go ahead. Let's get some information from people coming out of Rafah first."

But there was hardly anyone. And the rare ones who did turn up told us we were out of our minds and categorically advised us not to go one meter further. Eventually a young man appeared: he'd managed to get his sisters out of Rafah and bring them to Khan Younis by a roundabout route. A little later we saw him get into a car and drive off back to the bombarded town. Without asking anyone, my driver decided to follow him—he was fed up with all the hanging around and vacillating. The others followed us.

We managed to get to Rafah without any problem. But just as we were going into the town, the house we were driving past took the full force of a bomb. The *New York Times* photographer got out to take some photos, and we went to see a little hospital that was nearby. There were so many dead bodies there that they'd laid them out in the parking spaces. That hospital couldn't do much anyway—people were dying so quickly and in such large numbers. In the second hospital that we went to, the bodies were put in the fridges for fruit and vegetables, others were waiting outside in the courtyard. I saw a man coming with the body of his nine-year-old son in his arms. I asked him some questions, and he answered in a toneless voice. After that, I couldn't stand the stench of death any longer, I didn't have the heart to talk to the relatives of the victims, I had the feeling we were grave-robbers. I preferred to go and look for my father.

I phoned him, he answered. "I have no intention of moving, Asmaa, it's too dangerous."

"But we're a convoy of journalists, that gives us protection."

"I've told you: no question. I'm staying."

I kept badgering him, trying to convince him. Eventually he gave in and asked me to come by and pick him up. So we did head back with him. Immediately I could see that he was so terrorized he was in a state of shock, so I started telling him stories, any old stories, without stopping. As soon as he started talking about death and the imminent danger, I said to him, "But at least I'll die with you rather than all alone," and went right back to the meaningless story he'd interrupted: my uncles, the disagreements that kept us apart, the family conflicts, the children and so on until the moment when I could say to him, "Look, Papa, we're out of Rafah." In fact, we managed to get to Gaza without any hold-ups and where my mother welcomed us home with a huge sigh of relief.

34

A Million-Dollar Death

I WOKE UP AT 6:30 the following morning, August 3. On my cell phone I saw that the correspondent of the *Al Aqsa* channel had phoned me seven times. I rang back.

"Do the Al-Ghouls who live in the Yibna district belong to your family?" he asked.

"Yes, why?"

"They were bombarded. But don't worry, there were only four dead."

I went pale. We switched on the radio: it was my family, they were all sleeping in the house where I'd spent my childhood, that was now a pile of rubble. The number of victims rose to six, then to seven, eight, finally nine. We all started crying, wailing, my mother, my brothers...

And my father was still asleep! I went to wake him, telling him as gently as possible, "Papa, Uncle Ismael's house has been bombed..."

He opened one eye. "Did they fire a blank shell on the roof before bombing it?"

"No."

"That means they'll all be dead."

So we were woken to the catastrophe of which I'd had a premonition two days previously. The victims were my uncle, who was sixty, his wife, four of their children and three of their grandchildren, including the youngest, Mustafa, who was less than three months old. He was one of the twins who had recently been born in the family. But who could have decided that it was Mustafa who had died and Ibrahim who was alive? Who had been able to tell the one from the other, when their father had perished and their mother was in intensive care in the hospital? What doubt was this survivor going to have to take with him throughout his life?

This disturbing story of a double wasn't the only one, since one of my cousins who had been assassinated, Asmaa al-Ghoul, twenty-two years old, had the same name as me. My cousins, where had they gone? I thought about that all the time. I wrote a short story about it: "Where are they?" They hadn't enjoyed much pleasure on this earth, poverty-stricken as they were. None of them belonged to Hamas nor to any other political party. My Uncle Ismael was a very pragmatic person. He was a worker who used to buy stocks of clothes and resell them. He'd spent his life working in Israel and could speak Hebrew very well. It was his van I'd been behind when, as a child, I'd refused the sweet the soldier had offered me...

Two missiles launched by an F16 fighter had pulverized their house. It seems that just one of those missiles costs half a million dollars. They'd spent their whole life in poverty in that mean house—no foundations, no cement, no decoration, nothing at all, a corrugated-iron roof—and their death had cost a million dollars! What a bleak farce! May God have mercy on them.

Three weeks earlier, on the fourth day of the war, I had gone to Rafah in order to do some research on a family, the Ghannams, who had been the victims of a shell. I had put some pieces of chocolate in my pocket that I was going to give to my Grandmother Zakiya. On my way I passed the house of my childhood and had seen my Uncle Ismael sitting outside the door. I said hello and he invited me in, telling me that my other grandmother, Ghazaleh, was visiting them. Thus I happened to meet all those who were going to die. It was Ramadan, and they were preparing to break their fast. One of my cousins had taken refuge there with his wife and children because their own house was close to the area with the tunnels that was being heavily bombarded. I embraced them all as well as my cousins Asmaa and Hanadi. We laughed a lot—I'd started throwing the pieces of chocolate in the air, and the children were trying to catch them.

My uncle's wife came out of the kitchen saying, "I heard Asmaa's voice," and gave me a hug—"How did you come to be here, you crazy woman?"—and invited me to break my fast with them.

But I refused. "My mother will kill me, I have to go back to Gaza right away."

Then they told me they had a surprise for me and took me into a bedroom where I saw the twins born on the second day of the war, just forty-eight hours ago. I didn't know that I was saying farewell to them, to their parents, to everyone— as I was to the house in which I'd grown up and for the first time heard the BBC Arabic service which my grandfather always used to listen to as he went to sleep... May God have mercy on their souls.

Memories and words were jostling inside my head, in my throat, they were making me choke. The Internet was cut off, and I simply had to write. I went to a place on the beach, were I knew a connection was possible, and started, "I'm not going to stay silent. I'm not going to cry. I'm going to write, write until the end."

People seeing me from a distance came up to offer their condolences: I stopped for a while, cried a little then started to write again. Until I could get the article out from inside me that the foreign press was to take up widely: "Never talk to me about peace again." It was neither a slogan nor a wisecrack. I'd always thought that peace was the only thing that could resolve this conflict. But after having seen my family killed in that way—one of my cousins had woken up with a sore tummy and, when he touched it, found himself with his intestines in his hands; he'd called his father, then his brother and, getting no reply, had realized they were dead... When these appalling details of the death of your loved ones come to you, and you continue to see them in photos and videos, what kind of peace can you be talking about anymore? These are my own feelings I'm expressing, not some political stance. What peace when a missile falls on a family who are asleep and don't even know they're dying? And when their house, my house, that had been standing for sixty-three years and where I'd read my first book, is destroyed in the same second? I will never be in favor of war or violence. However ugly they are, I know that wars finish with peace between enemies. But that is a political peace, while what I'm talking about is inner peace.

There is one thing I still haven't understood: how the Israelis could approve of a government that kills human beings so coolly, how they could justify its actions. It's as if a general blindness had descended on the society, as if the bombardment of Gaza and its inhabitants simply wasn't happening. There are some, however, who have raised their voices and exerted great influence—for example, the reporter for the *Haaretz* newspaper, Gideon Levy, a great guy. No Arab has written like him! Fanatical Palestinians have asked for him to be silenced, persuaded he was a hypocrite: they simply couldn't believe that an Israeli could write such things. I followed his articles day after day, and I believe that his voice has unfortunately been neither sufficiently strong nor sufficiently heard. He's had so many threats he's been forced to employ a bodyguard. Since that's the way things are, I'd very much like him to come and live in Gaza. I've always refused requests for interviews from Radio Israel or other Israeli media. I just couldn't talk to them, I found it impossible. But if it had been Gideon Levy, how could I have said no?

35

Those Who Won the War

DURING THE FIRST WEEKS of the war, everyone supported Hamas, even its opponents, even me! People said, "To hell with Israel and the pseudo-peace they keep talking about." Then things changed. People all started to say the same thing at the same time, "That's enough, this war's gone on long enough, we want to have a life."

We could clearly see that the Arab world couldn't care less about Gaza and was in league against the Islamist government—which prompted a certain sympathy for it—but enough was enough. I posted on my Facebook page, "The Hamas leaders have to make a decision. If Israel is crazy, we don't have to be like that as well. We don't want to see our families killed any longer." I received such criticism for having dared to write those words. Even some of my friends came out against me.

"You're nothing but liars," I replied, "and I refuse to lie. I am for the resistance, but I'm also for the people and what I've written is what I've heard them saying: they don't want the war anymore, they need to be able to breathe again."

Your daughter's late, your heart sinks because you sense that something might have happened to her. What parent hasn't experienced that situation? Now just imagine that this sinking of your heart never stops, neither by day nor by night, for fifty days in a row. That's what we lived through:

our hearts gripped with fear as we waited, our children in danger, the bomb about to fall on them, God forbid, the missile launched by the plane, the shell at this moment, at the next, soon, at any moment... A short truce? We can't believe it's going to last and our anxiety is increased tenfold. Our hearts tell us, "That's it. This time we're going to die, it's our turn now."

This was the message from Israel, "We are capable of destroying Gaza and no one in the world will come to help you, no one will stop us, you are at our mercy."

And, indeed, the whole world let them go ahead. Who supported Gaza? Public opinion in Algeria and Egypt—with moderation; world opinion—a little; the UN, the NGOs, Great Britain... The biggest demonstration of support was in London, there were none in the Arab world—and the ones in Paris were forbidden! So it was true, the Israelis had a completely free hand.

Some Arab countries quietly thought that the defeat of Hamas would also mean the defeat of the Muslim Brotherhood and so they should let it happen. Conversely, some members of Hamas thought that the war would give new impetus to it and lead to its revival. In both cases, it was as if the people on whom the bombs were falling didn't exist. Trapped between these two 'opinions', we were heading for our destruction.

Living in this furnace, I simply didn't want to see the bombs falling on our heads anymore. But when the Israelis kill a family in the middle of a truce, like everyone else I want to send some rockets to them in return, telling them, "Our blood isn't as cheaply bought as you think." Their airmen see the houses from up in the sky and don't even imagine there are people sleeping in them. My uncle's family is just one example. You can't think logically in that situation, it would drive you mad. It's sickening to see innocent civilians killed like that, at the last minute. And when Hamas started to flex its muscles, the Israeli army withdrew to bombard the country even more savagely from outside. Eventually it was nothing but terrible air raids.

However, when the explosions fell quiet, I felt something was missing, everyone felt it, it was awful. Just as there are the *baby blues*—depression after giving birth—or depression at the start of winter, there's a post-war depression. When the conflict is at its height, fear and danger force you to face up to it, to protect yourself and your family, but afterward? You have nothing to do anymore, and it's at that moment that depression attacks you. And at the same time, people start to be afraid, profoundly afraid, that a fourth war might break out, and they still are today.

But who won what during that summer of 2014, and who lost? Hamas threw a stone at Israel, and Israel burnt Gaza down—that's the way things went. What have the Israelis gained? Their madness has made them lose world opinion for a long time—even if they don't care and believe that the United States is the sole support they need. On the other hand, Hamas gained nothing on the ground. At the finish, Gaza was in ruins and more hermetically sealed off than ever. Perhaps they had no 'political' goal anyway. I'm talking about Hamas per se but also about each one of its foot soldiers. For them to 'resist' is to 'fight in the field'—and they have achieved their goal. Mission accomplished. Some have fallen, others not, and the survivors have some stories to tell, memories of fighting and valor. That was their choice but certainly not that of the civilians who died under the bombardment. In six years we've had three wars against Israel, it's absolutely insane! I respect the 'resistance' and if they want to start a war, that's up to them, but not with our blood! Count me out this time. I love Gaza, but I also love my children. I refuse to let them live in permanent danger any longer. Hamas has a project that has nothing to do with me. It is due to the party's political tenacity that it's stayed in power. But it's crumbling in another way—like a balloon deflating—because people are no longer following it. We're all watching the sight of Hamas losing the struggle, despite all its obstinacy. It's perhaps sad for them, but we can't help feeling joy at the fall of a dictatorship. Everything comes to an end. There comes a time when everything that has had its day of glory no longer has it—just as Fatah came to its end. That's the course of history. Now Gaza is awaiting the great change, not knowing what it will bring.

But if we continue to judge Hamas in terms of our liberal beliefs, that will get us nowhere. The only result we'll get from calling them assassins and shutting them out will be to make them thrive. If it's free to come and go, a cat's still a cat, but if you close your doors and windows to it, it will turn into a furious tiger. It's only when the borders are open that people can travel around the world, see women, have money, discover the fantastic things this planet has to offer. A former Hamas minister of the interior said, and I was there, "We will free Europe from its corruption." The poor man really believed it! If he'd been to Europe just once it would have cured him of his stupidity.

So everybody lost, then? Not entirely. Since the guns have fallen silent, I see people coming out of their homes once more, couples walking down the street together laughing—even when they don't have a house any longer. They watch the new season of "Arab Idol" on TV and try to forget. They're fine! It was a war and it's over—and it's as if every war gave them a new life. The barrage of shells and missiles has taught them what survival means and how to live with pain and death right up to the very end. Seeing them like this, they look calm and relaxed, but that's just their way of resisting. Neither Israel nor Hamas has been able to take their lives away from them. We are the nation that takes the hardest knocks and that heals the quickest. We sometimes have wounds that go right to the bone, but we're back on our feet the next day thinking about an outing, make-up, love... The conservatives criticize us harshly for that. They don't understand that it's the life-affirming reaction of those who have looked death in the face. We want to live our lives as we have lived through death—to the extreme. Gaza has always been rebellious. No one has ever been able to govern it for more than twenty years. It's a crazy city, obstinate, addictive, I am her daughter, and I look like her. I am the one who won it, that war, and these are my children, the children of Gaza, because we're still alive and I'm wearing a red dress.